on track ...

Elvis Costello and The Attractions

every album, every song

Georg Purvis

sonicbondpublishing.com

Sonicbond Publishing Limited
www.sonicbondpublishing.co.uk
Email: info@sonicbondpublishing.co.uk

First Published in the United Kingdom 2021
First Published in the United States 2021

British Library Cataloguing in Publication Data:
A Catalogue record for this book is available from the British Library

ISBN 978-1-78952-129-0

Typeset in ITC Garamond & ITC Avant Garde
Printed and bound in England

Graphic design and typesetting: Full Moon Media

on track ...

Elvis Costello and The Attractions

every album, every song

Georg Purvis

sonicbondpublishing.com

Dedicated to David Moreau, who accompanied me to my first Elvis Costello concert at the Electric Factory in Philadelphia on 19 May 2007.

Without Whom …

This book is the culmination of nearly 20 years of appreciation, admiration, and (occasional) devotion for Elvis Costello. Thanks to Stephen Lambe for the opportunity to write this book, and for his immense passion and appreciation for good music.

Thanks to my friends and family who helped and supported me along the way: Scott Armstrong, Bob Bingaman, Noel Bartocci and Sam Costa, Raoul Caes and Jess Roth, Mark Costello, Mike Czawlytko and Julia Favorov, Jacob Carpenter, Tom Castagna, Joe and Danielle DeCarolis, Nick, Nikki and Mia DiBuono, Marissa Edelman, Rachael Edwards, Eileen Falchetta, Matt Gorzalski, Julia Green and Phil DeBiasio, Dave Grow and Michelle Scott, Betty and Chris Hackney, Jim, Louise, Penelope and Jordan Kent, Scott Koenig, JD Korejko and Su-Shan Jessica Lai, Kristen Kurtis, Steph Larson, Dan Lawler, John Malhman IV and Alessa Abruzzo, Brad McGinnis, Olivia Miller, Nick Prestileo, Billy and Annie Ransford, Patrick Remington and Beth Johnston, Heather Sailer, Kyra Schwartz and Syd Steinberg, Steve Sokolow, Eleni Solomos, John Dougherty and Valentina, Christine, Lillian and Everett Swing, Erin Tennity and Randy Richard, and Eric Zerbe. Additional thanks to Philip Brooks for advice, helping me through some tough times, and asking me if the book's done yet!

Special thanks to:

Lori, Hugh and Edward McGovern; my father, Georg; Patrice Babineau; my mother, Lynn; and my sister, Leah.

Steph Mlot, for being an eager pupil to an overzealous teacher (at least that's how I viewed it!) – and for the Sugarcanes' concert in Wolf Trap; Cameron Cuming, for being a willing sport and overall good egg (despite your insistence that *Goodbye Cruel World* is better than it actually is); Chelsea Bennett, for sharing the obsession, our many discussions on each successive EC album release and what we liked or didn't like, and humouring my drunken rendition of 'Beyond Belief' at your request; and Meredith McGovern, for your eternal love and support and for being a willing participant in this hobby of mine. I love you, my funny valentine.

on track ...

Elvis Costello

and The Attractions

Contents

Foreword

I first became aware of Elvis Costello in 1999, when three of my friends and I saw *Austin Powers: The Spy Who Shagged Me*, for my 16th birthday. I won't pretend I didn't find the movie hilarious, but I was going through something of a musical revelation at the time and was wildly impressed with the soundtrack: The Who, Lenny Kravitz – Green Day appealed to my teenage male sensibilities, while I harboured a secret appreciation of Madonna's 'Beautiful Stranger'. But it was the bizarre cameo appearance of Elvis Costello and Burt Bacharach in swingin' London circa 1969 that grabbed me. I had been peripherally aware of Costello, so much that I knew this collaboration with Bacharach was an anomaly, but nothing had compelled me to explore his music any further.

Sometime in April 2002, while walking around a Borders book store, I came across two CDs that captured my attention. The first appeared to be two large plastic cartoon bees, perhaps a child's toy at a carnival; the second was an intense-looking geek scowling at me over a Hasselblad camera. I bit the bullet and bought both. In my car, I put *This Year's Model* into the CD player first and was disappointed that I didn't immediately love it, having heard so much about it. I gave *When I Was Cruel* a chance instead, and that did it: I needed to get everything by this man. And so I did – but I wasn't much of a concert-goer at the time, and so it took me five years before I finally witnessed Elvis and his new backing band The Imposters (two-thirds of The Attractions with bassist Davey Faragher) live. From that moment forward I vowed to see him whenever I could, and I'm glad I did, because each successive concert has been a wildly different experience – and sometimes backing band – each time. If you're reading this and you haven't seen Elvis live yet, you absolutely must.

I'd wanted to write an Elvis Costello book for years, but I couldn't find the right angle. He's already written the definitive autobiography – twice: the first was between 1993 and 2005, as Rykodisc and, later, Rhino reissued his records on CD and included extensive self-penned liner notes that got as close to an autobiography that fans would get, until he published his autobiography – *Unfaithful Music and Disappearing Ink* – in 2015.

So I chose to whittle my focus down to Elvis Costello and his time with The Attractions, though two solo albums – *My Aim Is True* (1977) and *King of America* (1986) – are integral parts of the story and so are discussed. Additionally, I've opted not to discuss in depth The Attractions' brief reunion in the 1990s or the two albums they then featured on *Brutal Youth* and *All This Useless Beauty* – there's enough meat on that bone for an eventual follow-up.

One final note: Elvis was a fan of pseudonyms and *nom de plume*s – famously reverting to his birth name in 1985 – the instances of which are noted throughout the text when appropriate. For the sake of your sanity and mine, I address him as Declan in the introduction and first half of the first chapter to the point he became known professionally as Elvis Costello. From there, regardless of how he was credited, I refer to him by his professional name, except in the event of a quote, song credit, or personnel credit.

Introduction: Oh, I Just Don't Know Where To Begin...

Declan Patrick MacManus was born on 25 August 1954 to Ross and Lillian MacManus. His first record was The Beatles' *Please Please Me*, purchased by Ross for the nine-year-old. The following year, Declan used his own money to acquire Georgie Fame's *Fame at Last* EP.

This wasn't young Declan's first taste of music: his father was a trumpeter, vocalist, and bandleader; his mother, a record store manager. Throughout much of Declan's childhood, his father was the featured vocalist for the Joe Loss Orchestra (Britain's top big band), and a solo artist, scoring a minor hit with 'Patsy Girl' in Germany in 1966. Four years later, Ross – now going by Day Costello – achieved another hit single, this time in Australia, with The Beatles' 'The Long And Winding Road'.

Given his upbringing, Declan's fate as a musician was a given. His first commercially available performance was on Ross's jingle for R. White's Lemonade, where Declan sang backing vocals and played guitar. By this point, he had formed the acoustic duo, Rusty, with his school friend, Allan Mayes, thus being exposed to the thrill of an enraptured audience, as well as the downsides of the music industry: the two might earn up to £10 a night, but it was more common that they would walk away with nothing.

By the end of 1972, Declan was living in with his mother in Liverpool and – despite recording a six-track demo with Mayes – decided that the music scene was too limited and upped sticks to London to live with his father, by now remarried. He also needed money and got a job as a computer operator at the Elizabeth Arden factory in Acton; it was menial work ('My duties included printing out invoices for the moustache waxes of the occasional Duchess who visited the company's West End salon. Some of the work was more tedious'), often completed quickly and without much supervision, so he spent most of his time honing his songwriting skills.

In mid-1973, Declan discovered the pub rock band Brinsley Schwarz and hit it off with two fellow fans, Mich Kent and Malcolm Dennis. The three had several common music interests (The Band, Little Feat, Gram Parsons, Grateful Dead and Joni Mitchell) and were struggling musicians – Kent a bassist, Dennis a drummer. Before long, Dickie Faulkner (congas) and Steve Hazlehurst (guitar, vocals) joined. (Dennis left in early 1975 after a punch-up with Declan; Ian Powling replaced Dennis on drums.). A name was needed, and after The Mothertruckers and The Bizzario Brothers were (rightly) rejected, Declan's fiancé Mary Burgoyne suggested Flip City: inspired by Cheech Marin babbling away ('Man, the chick is twisted, crazy, poop-shoobie, y'hear? Flip city!') on the spoken word section of Joni Mitchell's 'Twisted' from her *Court and Spark* album.

Declan took charge of the songwriting for Flip City, but it soon became apparent that his aspirations didn't match those of his bandmates: they found

Flip City to be a fun lark, but Declan was more preoccupied with making money. It's hard to fault him: despite making a living wage at Elizabeth Arden, he and Mary, now married, were proud parents to Matthew but still found it tough to make ends meet. Instead of taking on a promotion or a better-paying job, Declan pushed ahead with his musical aspirations, though they still had to downgrade, first by taking on some roommates who were of questionable renown. The situation got so dire that they had to move in with Mary's parents near Heathrow airport, though Declan's commute would inspire several of his new songs.

By the end of December 1975, Flip City was no more, and Declan was ready to make a go of it on his own. Before long, he had recorded a tape full of original compositions that he was schlepping around to largely disinterested record executives, who nonetheless humoured him anyway and let him perform some of the songs in-office. After receiving little feedback from any of the prospects (and being offered a deal from Island Records, which he found so insulting that he rejected it outright), Declan read an advertisement for the newly-formed Stiff Records and its founders, Jake Riviera and Dave Robinson. Their expanding roster included The Pink Fairies, The Damned and Nick Lowe: former Brinsley Schwarz member and an early inspiration of Declan's, so it came as a pleasant coincidence when the two happened to run into each other while he was returning from the Stiff Records offices. Though they had first met back in 1972 – when Lowe had been impressed with Declan's musical ambitions – there hadn't been any contact since. Four years later, the two caught up, with Declan mentioning to Lowe the tape he had just dropped off at Stiff. The two went their separate ways, but it was not to be their final meeting.

My Aim Is True (1977)

Personnel:
Elvis Costello: vocals, guitar; piano and drumstick on 'Mystery Dance'
John McFee: guitar, pedal steel guitar
Sean Hopper: keyboards, backing vocals
Johnny Ciambotti: bass guitar, backing vocals
Mickey Shine: drums
Nick Lowe: backing vocals; bass, piano, and drumstick on 'Mystery Dance'
Stan Shaw: organ on 'Less Than Zero'
Recorded at Pathway Studios, London, late 1976–early 1977
Produced by Nick Lowe
UK release date: 22 July 1977; US release date: March 1978
Highest chart places: UK: 14, US: 32
Running time: 32:31

At Stiff Records, the response to Declan's tape was promising, and he was repeatedly called in during the subsequent few weeks to meet with various personnel. He impressed the managers of the fledgeling label enough that they signed him to Stiff (as D. P. Costello: his new surname a nod to his paternal great-grandmother's maiden name) in August 1976. At first, it was suggested that Declan only write material for other artists – primarily Dave Edmunds – but, not content with being pigeonholed as a songwriter, Declan continued to write and record demos at an alarming rate. (It was even suggested that he share an album with fellow Stiff label-mate, Wreckless Eric, though this idea was scuppered.) Finally, Riviera and Robinson were convinced that Declan should be the one to sing his own songs, and the notion of writing songs for other artists was silently put to bed.

In October 1976, Declan was introduced to the musicians who would be the backing band on his first record. Clover were a California-based band who had been coaxed over to England by Riviera. With several albums already under their belt, they proved to be the perfect musical foil for the songs that Declan was writing and helped define his early pub rock sound (though it would be completely obliterated and revamped by the formation of The Attractions the following summer). What was even more incidental was that Declan was a fan of Clover – certainly, he was drawn to their country-rock flavour, much as he was to the Grateful Dead and The Flying Burrito Brothers, among others – and had performed a handful of their songs while in Flip City. Declan and the musicians – which included John McFee on pedal steel guitar, Sean Hopper on keyboards and backing vocals, Johnny Ciambotti on bass guitar, and Mickey Shine on drums – along with producer Nick Lowe, would rehearse the songs at Headley Grange during the day, then go to Pathway Studios in Islington at night to record them. In all, the album took sixteen hours to record and five hours to mix, at a cost of less than £1,000.

'Simplicity' was the word of the day, and such luxuries as overdubs or elaborate arrangements were out of the question. The basic goal was to commit the songs to plastic without too much fuss or hassle. Lowe was manning the control room with Roger Bechirian engineering, and it proved to be a perfect pairing. Lowe had little technical knowledge – leaving the complicated stuff to Bechirian – preferring to capture the initial feel and raw energy of a song instead of producing it to death. This, along with the tiny confines of Pathway Studios, gave the music its distinctive gritty sound that sat neatly as a mix somewhere between pub rock and punk.

The album was finally completed in January 1977, with Declan having used up a considerable amount of sick days to record it. He couldn't yet afford to quit his day job – and wouldn't be able to until the summer of 1977, nearly a year after he was signed to Stiff (his signing bonus was £150, a tape recorder, and a battery-powered guitar amplifier) – but he became a kind of unofficial Stiff employee, stopping by on the way home from work to help with ad campaigns and slogans.

With the initial plan of recording a single ('Radio Sweetheart' backed with 'Mystery Dance') now pushed aside in favour of a full-length album, a drastic change was needed. The name Declan MacManus hardly threatened the newest class of musicians who had names like Rat Scabies, Captain Sensible, and Sid Vicious; D. P. Costello, the name Declan used on his demo tapes (a nod to his father and great-grandmother), was little better. His managers insisted that he change his name to something bold, drastic, guaranteed to create controversy and even incite a little bit of anger.

Elvis Presley was still very much a beloved musical icon, though, by early 1977, he was in terminal decline due to years of drug abuse. The once iconic legend was bordering on bloated self-parody, with his concerts now incoherent messes, though his irregular stream of singles still managed to perform well in the country charts. All the same, nobody had any idea how ill he was or that he would soon pass away.

Declan had adapted a confrontational approach to his own performances – a friend recalled to biographer Graeme Thomson, that 'he was intense, utterly focused and single-minded; he didn't suffer fools gladly' – which Riviera and Robinson had noticed. Having already reinvented himself on his demo tapes, Declan decided to stick with Costello as his surname (insisting it was pronounced 'COS-tello', instead of the more familiar 'Cos-TELL-o'; eventually, he gave in, and the latter pronunciation stuck) while Riviera insisted his new Christian name be Elvis; Clover bassist Johnny Ciambotti recalled Riviera bursting into the studio during a session and shouting, 'Elvis! That's it – Elvis!', while, according to Thomson, the more accepted legend is that 'the change of name took place during a drunken meeting in a restaurant on the Fulham Road early in 1977'. Even Costello wasn't sure of the new name: 'Jake and Dave would come at you like good-cop/bad-cop', he recalled. "This'll be great", Jake just said, "We're going to call you Elvis. Ha ha ha ha!".

And I thought it was just one of these mad things that would pass off, and of course, it didn't. Then it became a matter of honour as to whether we could carry it off'.

However it was decided upon, the new name was met with a mixed reaction. Charlie Gillett – the man who had played Declan's early demos on his radio program – was furious over what he considered a betrayal. Others found it funny, while most US critics were outraged, thinking it a slight against their own beloved Elvis. 'It wasn't meant as an insult to (him)', Costello explained in late 1977. 'It's unfortunate if anyone thinks we're having a go at him in any way.' Those who were quick to clutch their pearls were obviously unaware of the timeline of events: Costello's first single, 'Less Than Zero', was issued in March 1977, five months before Presley would be dead in the middle of August.

With the new name change came a change of image as well: Costello was given a pair of comically oversized horn-rimmed spectacles and dressed in the finest thrift shop threads. It was an iconic image that has been preserved on the cover of his debut album *My Aim Is True* (titled after a key line in the torch song of the record, 'Alison'): clutching his Fender Jazzmaster as if he were brandishing a shotgun, Costello smirks at the camera, knock-kneed and flat-footed. It wasn't meant to be menacing, but there was something uneasy about the photo. One critic famously said about Costello; 'This fellow looked like he'd find it hard to aim a paper airplane'.

Stiff went into Costello overdrive, with one of their marketing ploys to get him some much-needed attention: the 'Help Us Hype Elvis' campaign began with the single release of '(The Angels Wanna Wear My) Red Shoes', with the slogan etched into the A-side's runoff groove. Stiff's in-house artist, Barney Bubbles, then constructed a form for the first 1,000 copies of *My Aim Is True* to be released in the UK, where the purchaser of the album could fill out the form, send it into Stiff Records, and a free copy would be sent to a friend. Whether it was a success has not been confirmed, though the album's eventual success meant that some of the promotion must have worked. Besides, who doesn't like to be threatened into liking new musicians?

The album's release was delayed until July 1977 due to distribution disputes between Stiff and Island Records. The momentum was lost on the record-buying public, and the album's first three singles – 'Less Than Zero', 'Alison', and '(The Angels Wanna Wear My) Red Shoes' – all, well, stiffed in the UK charts. The album itself performed rather well eventually, reaching number 14 in the UK (not bad for a debut), but now Elvis was ready to promote it. He just needed a band – again.

'Welcome To The Working Week' (Elvis Costello)

B-side of 'Alison', 27 May 1977.

It's fitting that the first song on Elvis's first album was titled 'Welcome To The Working Week'. Written – along with most of *My Aim Is True* – while commuting to his day job at Elizabeth Arden, the song takes aim at the next year's model ('Now that your picture's in the paper bein' rhythmically admired') and the shallowness of the fashion world. In a contemporary interview, he sneered, 'There's nothin' glamorous or romantic about the world at the moment', and he would view that world through the eyes of a sexually frustrated suburban working drone who doesn't view her modelling profession as a career, but instead as a means for self-gratification.

'Miracle Man' (Elvis Costello)

This song found its origins in 'Baseball Heroes': a track Elvis wrote and recorded with Flip City in 1974, though he later admitted that writing about the primarily American pastime was out of his league and continued to tweak the words, ending up with the song's final title by the time Flip City disbanded. Still believing the song had promise, Elvis discarded most of the original lyric – apart from the newly-written chorus: 'You know that walking on water won't make you a miracle man' – and cooked up the story of a male narrator in an unhappy relationship with a verbally abusive and dismissive woman. Not only is the song about a man who's 'doing everything just trying to please her/Even crawling around on all fours', but it also portrays him as sexually impotent, which the woman doesn't shy away from reminding him about: 'Why do you have to say that there's someone who can do it better than I can?'.

'No Dancing' (Elvis Costello)

Continuing the previous song's subject of an impotent man in a relationship with a domineering woman, 'No Dancing' is written from the viewpoint of a casual observer. At first, the narrator sympathises with the man – who has been made to look like a fool by his woman – but rescinds his support in the second verse upon revealing the man's mundane life ('He's such a drag/He's not insane/It's just that everybody has to feel his pain'), almost like that of a sex-deprived Walter Mitty.

'Blame It On Cain' (Elvis Costello)

Live recording B-side of 'Watching The Detectives', 14 October 1977.

In the Bible, Cain – the first-born son of Adam and Eve – is a land cultivator, and his younger brother, Abel, is a shepherd. Angered by God's admiration of Abel while receiving no divine acknowledgements of his own, Cain takes his brother out to a field and mercilessly slaughters him, thus becoming history's first murderer. 'Blame It On Cain' has nothing to do with that; instead, Elvis' narrator is besieged by financial woes, and he's willing to do whatever it takes to keep himself and his partner afloat.

Another perfunctory pub rocker, 'Blame It On Cain' earned its wings in the live setting, though a fairly tentative version from 7 August 1977 was released on the double B-side of 'Watching The Detectives'. ('Mystery Dance', from the same concert, was the other B-side.)

'Alison' (Elvis Costello)

A-side, 27 May 1977.

Unlike the rest of *My Aim Is True*, 'Alison' was written not on his way to work, but at home after his wife and young son had drifted off to sleep ('I didn't really know what they sounded like until I got into the studio', he later wrote). As for who Alison was?: 'I've always told people that I wrote the song after seeing a beautiful checkout girl at the local supermarket', he wrote in his autobiography, *Unfaithful Music and Disappearing Ink*:

> She had a face for which a ship might have once been named. Scoundrels might once have fought mist-swathed duels to defend her honour. Now she was punching in the prices on cans of beans at a cash register and looking as if all the hopes and dreams of her youth were draining away. All that were left would soon be squandered to a ruffian who told her convenient lies and trapped her still further. I was daydreaming… Again…

Elvis goes into pretty specific detail about the song in his autobiography, and it's worth reading uninterrupted, but the most telling assessment he made was that 'it was a premonition, my fear that I would not be faithful or that my disbelief in happy endings would lead me to kill the love that I had longed for'. Indeed, the Live Stiffs tour shortly after the release of *My Aim Is True* would begin the prolonged unravelling of his personal life.

Released as the second single from the album in May 1977 – with 'Welcome To The Working Week' as the B-side – 'Alison' failed to attract any attention in the charts. (The US single mix added syrupy strings, much to Elvis's annoyance.) It wasn't until Linda Ronstadt covered 'Alison' on her 1978 album *Living In the USA* that the song's status finally started to rise; while Elvis was especially dismissive of her recording, he admitted in 1998 that 'I didn't mind spending the money that she earned me'. Funnily enough, Ronstadt understood where Elvis was coming from: 'If you do something and then you see someone else doing it, you think like they are taking away part of your identity. It's a sensitive reaction; I've done it myself. And I took it for what it was back then. But I love Elvis. He writes like an old-fashioned songwriter. His songs are so beautifully tragic and they have a lot of meaning behind them. He's a gentleman, and he's got a great heart'.

'Sneaky Feelings' (Elvis Costello)

More pub-rock-meets-Randy-Newman, 'Sneaky Feelings' is one of the slighter tracks on *My Aim Is True*, cruising along at a jaunty pace while Elvis croons about disintegrating relationships. The song is enjoyable if unspectacular, though a quicker fade-out of the final minute – which drags on while Elvis repeats 'Oh, I've still got a long way to go' – would have been appreciated.

'(The Angels Wanna Wear My) Red Shoes' (Elvis Costello)

A-side, 7 July 1977.

On the surface, '(The Angels Wanna Wear My) Red Shoes' is a simple song, one that Elvis explained as being 'written on the Inter-City train to Liverpool between Runcorn and Lime Street stations, a journey of about 10 minutes. I had to keep the song in my head until I got to my mother's house, where I kept an old Spanish guitar that I had had since I was a kid. The lyric is a funny notion for a 22-year-old to have written'. Indeed, the complexity of the words may be overlooked upon first listen. It's easy to imagine the narrator as Elvis himself, a pigeon-toed, geeky and gawky young guy watching the girl – with whom he came to the dance and who left him stranded – while she flirts with more attractive men.

Musically, the song owes an obvious debt to The Byrds and Graham Parker & the Rumour, with its jangly guitar intro and surprisingly atypical vocal harmonies: notably, the sarcastic response vocals in the second chorus. The final coda is exciting, with Clover raging away as Elvis half-sneers and half-croons, 'Red shoes, the angels wanna wear my red shoes', as the recording fades away.

Released as the third single from *My Aim Is True* on 7 July 1977 – merely a week before The Attractions were formed – '(The Angels Wanna Wear My) Red Shoes' followed the leads of 'Less Than Zero' and 'Alison' by failing to chart. Hopes that this single would be Elvis' breakthrough chart success were dashed, but not for long; it turned out he just needed the right band to guide him there.

'Less Than Zero' (Elvis Costello)

A-side, 25 March 1977.

During recording sessions for *My Aim Is True*, Elvis happened to watch a BBC programme which interviewed 'the despicable Oswald Mosley ... The former leader of the British Union of Fascists seemed unrepentant about his poisonous actions of the 1930s', Elvis later seethed. Mosley had modelled himself after Benito Mussolini and took particular offence at Jewish residents of Britain, demanding that they either renounce their heritage or be deported from the country. He attempted to organise a march through an area with a high population of Jewish residents (subsequently known as the Battle of Cable Street), but thousands of protesters of Mosley's viewpoint prevented the march from taking place. The effect was profound enough for the country to enact the Public Order of 1936, which banned political uniforms and quasi-military-style organisations.

Elvis was so disgusted with the almost romantic reminiscing that Mosley displayed that he promptly wrote a new song that 'was more of a slandering fantasy than a reasoned argument'. Indeed, he loaded up his descriptive shotgun and blasted Mosley's character with a laundry list of misdeeds: sadism, brutality, paedophilia, incest, salaciousness and murder. Although Mosley hadn't been known to participate in any of these crimes – other than adultery, which was conspicuously absent from the list – Elvis cast the leader as the embodiment of corruption. Additionally, he condemned not only Mosley's horrendous acts but also the media for glorifying them, as evidenced in the chorus: 'Turn up the TV, No one listening will suspect' strongly suggests that the media is ready and willing to conceal the corruption of all politicians – implying that anyone rich and powerful enough can get away with just about anything – while desensitising viewers from the harsh glare of reality. Forty years on, and not much has changed.

Bassist Johnny Ciambotti was convinced that the 'Mr. Oswald' referred to Lee Harvey Oswald and the assassination of John F. Kennedy: especially the line 'A pistol was still smoking, a man lay on the floor/Mr. Oswald said he had an understanding with the law'. One night, Ciambotti explained his interpretation to Elvis, who was so inspired by this new slant, that he wrote a completely different version. Suitably known as the 'Dallas version' of 'Less Than Zero', Elvis never got around to recording it in the studio, though it supplanted the original version in the live setting almost immediately.

'Less Than Zero' was released as Elvis's first single in March 1977, and while it was an ambitious and strong composition, its blatant political overtones – coupled with its controversial list of misdeeds – made it a poor choice for the hit parade. The public certainly thought so, and the single failed to chart at all in the UK.

'Mystery Dance' (Elvis Costello)

B-side of '(The Angels Wanna Wear My) Red Shoes', 7 July 1977.

More often than not, whenever Elvis sang of dancing, on *My Aim Is True*, it was a not-so-subtle euphemism for fornication. So it's no surprise that having already tackled the issue of an impotent man stuck in a loveless relationship on 'Miracle Man' and 'No Dancing', he brings everything full circle with 'Mystery Dance', a song that sounds like a deranged 1950s rock/doo-wop pastiche that could have been covered by Elvis the first. The story is an ode to a couple's first sexual encounter, with each as clueless about how to begin the proceedings as the other: 'She thought that I knew, and I thought that she knew/So both of us were willing, but we didn't know how to do it'. Fittingly, the song is over in a brief 98 seconds, making the repeated 'I can't do it anymore and I'm not satisfied' all the more appropriate.

'Pay It Back' (Elvis Costello)

While Elvis was mostly careful to paper over his pub rock roots on *My Aim Is True*, he was unable to do so on 'Pay It Back', a lacklustre thumper written in the waning days of Flip City. At least the story is compelling: a man is trapped in a relationship because of an unexpected pregnancy, though he tries his hardest to be honest ('I wouldn't say that I was raised on romance/Let's not get stuck in the past'), before exclaiming to his girlfriend, 'I love you more than anything in the world'. Before she gets comfortable with this unexpected outburst of romance, he's quick to deliver the killer blow: 'I don't expect that will last'.

'I'm Not Angry' (Elvis Costello)

Lazy journalism often points at 'I'm Not Angry' as Elvis's first declaration of anger, but this (incorrectly) assumes that Elvis is writing about himself. In fact, fans and critics alike would often try to create parallels with characters in Elvis's songs that were either clearly fictitious creations or fabricated and distorted truths, done so to protect the innocent and guilty alike. 'I'm Not Angry' falls into the former category: the narrator is left to listen to an ex-girlfriend's romantic encounter, done so in retribution, and all he can muster is a half-hearted shrug. Then again, he sure doesn't sound like he's over it, with Elvis's sneering vocal delivery (matched in ferocity by John McFee's snaking guitar), and methinks he doth protest his lack of anger too much in the last 50 seconds as the song fades out.

'Waiting For The End Of The World' (Elvis Costello)

Original album closer 'Waiting for the End of the World' was inspired by Elvis's daily travels to and from work on the Underground: 'a fantasy based on a real late-night journey'. This Dylan-esque rant throws a cast of train car characters into disarray by 'pulling the hysteria out of newspaper headlines into the everyday boredom of the commuter'. Meanwhile, Clover's plodding arrangement – Mickey Shine's drums alone are apocalyptic – works to the song's benefit, as John McFee's pedal steel guitar snakes and slithers through Elvis' verses and choruses. A fitting conclusion, the song's power has since been diminished with 'Watching The Detectives' being retroactively promoted to album closer.

Related Tracks

'Radio Sweetheart' (Elvis Costello)

B-side of 'Less Than Zero', 25 March 1977.

Originally planned as Elvis' debut single, 'Radio Sweetheart' would likely have ended his career before it even started – or, more charitably, his career trajectory would have been significantly altered. 'Radio Sweetheart' isn't a bad song – far from it, with its clever wordplay and sprightly arrangement – but it was so out of touch with the musical landscape of 1977 and what Elvis would go on to do with The Attractions that its eventual home as the B-side of 'Less Than Zero' was for the best.

'Watching The Detectives' (Elvis Costello)

A-side, 14 October 1977; Peak position: 15.

A clatter of drums, a dub-inspired bass line, a vaguely jerky rhythm (not quite reggae, but a white English approximation thereof) are followed by one of the most instantly recognisable guitar riffs of Elvis Costello's career – and all in the span of twenty seconds. 'Watching The Detectives' has achieved wide acclaim in Elvis' career, and in the autumn of 1977, even became his first charting single. But its beginnings were certainly inauspicious: written in his front room in Whitton, 'fuelled by nothing stronger than a jar of instant coffee after repeatedly listening to the first album by The Clash', Elvis marvelled at that album's production and wanted to do something similar. 'Somewhere around dawn, the 'Watching The Detectives' story came into my mind. There were no barricades to mount in suburbia, no threat of riot, no hint of discontent.'

Elvis just so happened to have this song ready during auditions for his new backing band. Having played 'Alison' and 'Less Than Zero' endlessly with each candidate, Elvis broke up the monotony by teaching his borrowed support musicians – Graham Parker's rhythm section Andrew Bodnar and Steve Goulding – this new song. Impressed with what he heard, Nick Lowe booked a session at Pathway Studios, eager to capture the song as quickly as possible. He had his own vision for the song, and ran the mics 'hot' to get the massive distortion in the introduction. Elvis later noted, 'it was obvious from the first playback of 'Detectives' that this song was the real beginning of making records as opposed to just recording some songs in a room'. (Newly-hired keyboardist Steve Nason was called upon for keyboard overdubs; his Bernard Herrmann-inspired Vox Continental organ stabs were exactly what Elvis was looking for.)

Released as a non-album single in October 1977, 'Watching The Detectives' – backed with live recordings of 'Blame It On Cain' and 'Mystery Dance' (the first Attractions performances to be released on vinyl) – soared to fifteen in the UK, rewarding Stiff Records with their first Top Twenty single chart entry.

'Stranger In The House' (Elvis Costello)

A-side, 17 March 1978.

This outcast from the *My Aim Is True* sessions snuck out as a non-album bonus single with the first 50,000 copies of *This Year's Model.* While more charitable fans would contest that this was due to Elvis wanting to give an extra bang for the buck, it's just as equally a shrewd marketing ploy on Stiff Records' behalf to drum up more sales of the new record. As with 'Radio Sweetheart', 'Stranger In The House' was intended for his debut album, though Elvis (correctly) reasoned that 'including a country ballad was not thought to be a smart move in 1977'.

That didn't stop the managers of country and western legend, George Jones, from suggesting that he and Elvis record a duet, with a recording session planned for July 1978. 'Rumour had it that he was down in Florence, Alabama, and couldn't come into the state, as one of his more famous exes was looking for alimony', Elvis later wrote. 'But maybe they told me this just to give me a taste of the Nashville soap opera mythology and make me feel better about making the trip in vain.' The two finally recorded their vocal parts eight months later, and 'Stranger In The House' became a highlight of Jones's 1980 album *My Very Special Guests*.

'Neat Neat Neat' (live) (Brian James)
Live recording B-side of 'Stranger In The House', 17 March 1978.
Originally recorded by The Damned and released as their second single in February 1977, Elvis and The Attractions (with Davey Payne on saxophone) included a live version of this song in their setlist on 22 October 1977, dedicated to Chris Miller (real name of Damned drummer Rat Scabies) who had just gotten into a scrape in London. Much like The Who extending a gesture of solidarity toward the incarcerated Mick Jagger and Keith Richards in the summer of 1967 (by recording 'The Last Time' and 'Under My Thumb'), Elvis' intentions were good, though the song ultimately amounts to a loud-sounding nothing, bathed in echo. This performance was later released as the B-side of the 'Stranger In The House' free giveaway single.

This Year's Model (1978)

Personnel:
Elvis Costello: vocals, guitar
Steve Nieve: keyboards
Pete Thomas: drums
Bruce Thomas: bass guitar
Recorded at Eden Studios London, November 1977-January 1978
Produced by Nick Lowe
UK release date: 17 March 1978; US release date: May 1978
Highest chart places: UK: 4, US: 30
Running time: 35:58

Almost as soon as *My Aim Is True* had been released, Elvis was both auditioning his new band and writing songs for his next album. Clover was unable – or unwilling – to become Elvis' backing band, and the idea to commandeer Graham Parker's rhythm section (Andrew Bodnar and Steve Goulding) was discussed but never acted upon. Elvis would still use Bodnar and Goulding to help audition prospective band members, though the drummer's stool wasn't vacant for long: Elvis had been impressed with drummer Pete Thomas, who first played with Chilli Willi and The Red Hot Peppers until 1975, and was filling time as the drummer in John Stewart's band in Los Angeles. Riviera had also been the manager of Chilli Willi and convinced Pete to return to England to work with Wilko Johnson, formerly of Dr Feelgood. It turned out to be a ruse: Riviera used Johnson as a way to get another record company to pay for Pete's transatlantic flight. Within a week of his return, Pete became the drummer in Elvis' new band.

For the other two vacancies, an ad was placed in *Melody Maker* on 4 June 1977: 'Stiff Records Require Organist/Synthesiser Player and Bass Player – both able to sing for rocking pop combo. Must be broad-minded. Young or old'. One of the first bassists to call up the offices to apply was Bruce Thomas, who had an impressive resume: he had first worked with Paul Rodgers in The Roadrunners in 1967, before moving on to such bands as Bodast (with Steve Howe) and Quiver (with Tim Renwick), even recording with Al Stewart. Elvis was hesitant but was eventually convinced by Stiff's secretary to give Bruce a chance; with his first choice, Paul 'Bassman' Riley (Pete's fellow Chilli Willi bandmate), unavailable to join a band at the moment, Elvis conceded to an audition with Bruce, who purchased all of Elvis' singles and learned them note-for-note, but wasn't quite as sure-footed when he launched into two unrecorded songs, 'No Action' and 'Watching The Detectives'. Elvis recognised Bruce's 'fondness for venturing up the neck of his instrument to registers unfamiliar to other bass players', and hired him.

The only remaining position to fill was the keyboardist. Elvis was determined to only have one guitarist – himself – with the other musicians filling out the sound. After auditioning several keyboardists to no success, Steve Nason showed up and 'was easily the most impressive candidate at the auditions. He had asked to stay to hear the other players and later been discovered curled up asleep among the amplifiers, having quietly demolished a bottle of sweet cooking sherry'. Nason was quickly rechristened Steve Naïve but eventually evolved to Steve Nieve while on the Live Stiffs tour after he innocently asked what a groupie was.

The newly-formed quartet set about performing a handful of shows throughout the summer of 1977, though the band were still gaining their confidence, so the shows were largely haphazard. Elvis and his manager, Jake Riviera, were confident that success was just around the corner – but a little nudge to speed things up never hurt anyone: while UK sales of *My Aim Is True* were encouraging, Elvis desperately wanted a North American distributor to break into a wider market. It just so happened that a CBS Records convention was taking place at the Hilton Hotel in Mayfair on the night of The Attractions' London debut. It couldn't have been more perfect. Riviera convinced Elvis to play a solo gig outside the hotel, and so he plugged his guitar into a battery-powered amplifier and started into his repertoire, made up entirely of material from his new album. Though the CBS executives who walked out into the summer afternoon enjoyed themselves, the Hilton's staff weren't pleased with the disruption and called the police. Elvis was charged with busking, though he wouldn't go down without a fight: 'The senior inspector ... stood directly between me and my bemused audience'. he later wrote. 'He cautioned me that I was obstructing the footpath, although the opposite was clearly the truth. I took a step to the left. He did likewise. I took a step to the right. He followed suit and said, 'Do that again and you're nicked'. I could see in his eyes that he did not believe that I was about to turn on my heel. So I was arrested while all the other 'protesters' got clean away.'

The arrest did little to quell his pre-show jitters: as soon as he was detained, he informed the officers that he was supposed to make his London debut that evening. 'Not if we keep you in, sonny', he later recalled one saying. While he waited in a jail cell, news had spread back to Stiff Records that their newest star had been arrested; Elvis's solicitor phoned the police and, 'I don't know what was said, but suddenly I was given a cup of tea, they completed the paperwork, and the desperado was released'. Elvis was charged with 'selling records in the street' and fined £5 (£28 in today's money), which he couldn't afford. For all his troubles, it was a huge consolation that the controversy worked: Elvis was eventually signed to Columbia Records in October, with the US release of *My Aim Is True* following five months later.

The Attractions embarked on a gruelling tour of England between August and October before setting off for the United States in November. It was during the Stateside tour that Elvis refined the material for his next album. Just as quickly as the songs were written, they were performed live; what better way to rehearse material for a new album than on the road? This level of preparation worked to the band's benefit: *This Year's Model* was recorded in eleven days that November.

It also spoke to a deeper problem: Stiff Records was running Elvis and The Attractions ragged. When they weren't on tour, they were recording BBC radio sessions, filming music videos, or being shuffled off to *Top of the Pops* or interviewed for a music rag. Elvis later admitted that the constant touring – especially of North America – was taxing, but it benefited The Attractions: before long, their early haphazard shows were just a memory, and Elvis was later proud to recall that the number of poor Attractions shows could be counted on one hand.

Elvis and The Attractions finished up the year with another tour of the United States, this time appearing on the still-fresh primetime TV sketch show, *Saturday Night Live*. Hastily replacing the Sex Pistols – who couldn't get working visas in time to appear on the show – Elvis was less than thrilled when he was told to perform 'Less Than Zero'. With its narrative about Oswald Mosley, the former leader of the British Union of Fascists, Elvis protested that the song would make little sense to American viewers. Columbia Records told him in no uncertain terms that he was to play the song and that was that. Obviously, this didn't sit well with Elvis, though he initially played along: he and the Attractions ran through both 'Watching The Detectives' and 'Less Than Zero' at rehearsals, and when it was time for their second appearance (after playing the former song earlier in the show), Elvis led the band through the song for nearly eight seconds before he turned around, flailed his arms and shouted, 'Stop! Stop!'. He then spun back around and looked dead into the camera and said, 'I'm sorry, ladies and gentlemen. There's no reason to do this song here', turned back around and cued The Attractions for 'Radio, Radio': an as-yet-unreleased song he had written as a diatribe against the corporate world and biting the hand that feeds.

There was little choice but to let the stunt proceed. Elvis later explained he had seen the Jimi Hendrix Experience do something similar years earlier, when they appeared on the BBC show, *A Lulu Happening*. Scheduled to play 'Hey Joe', they obliged for a few seconds before Hendrix stopped the band and said, 'We'd like to stop playing this rubbish and dedicate a song to the Cream regardless of what kind of group they might be. I'd like to dedicate this to Eric Clapton, Ginger Baker, and Jack Bruce' before launching into an instrumental rendition of 'Sunshine Of Your Love'. It was this kind of spontaneity that Elvis wanted to spring upon *Saturday Night Live*, later joking that, 'Evidently, it's not that live'.

Upon its release in March 1978, *This Year's Model* received almost universal praise. *NME* called it 'too dazzling, too powerful to be ignored', while *Melody Maker* said the album 'promotes its author to the foremost ranks of contemporary rock writers'. The album flew to number 4 in the UK and 30 in the US: an astonishing feat for an artist's second album. But Elvis and The Attractions had little time to celebrate: they would play nearly 200 concerts in 1978 alone and were somehow able to squeeze in sessions for their third album during all that. It was a superhuman feat by any stretch of the imagination, though it became clear soon enough that such a schedule was bound to have its drawbacks.

'No Action' (Elvis Costello)

Opening Elvis' sophomore album and serving as the debut of The Attractions, 'No Action' is a frenetic and impressive statement. It starts off with Elvis on his own, sneering, 'I don't want to kiss you/I don't wanna touch' before The Attractions kick in and transform the song into the closest Elvis would ever get to punk.

But 'No Action' started life as another standard pub rocker, first recorded during the 'Watching The Detectives' sessions while Elvis, Andrew Bodnar, and Steve Goulding were rehearsing keyboardists. This early version, long available on various *My Aim Is True* reissues, is lugubrious and leaden, with Goulding's drums plodding and drenched in reverb. It took The Attractions to bring the subtleties to life, with Pete Thomas especially transforming the song with his urgent drumming, tinkling on his ride cymbal to emulate a phone ringing ('I'm not a telephone junkie'), and concluding the song with a rapid-fire drum solo.

'This Year's Girl' (Elvis Costello)

While touring North America in 1977, Elvis and The Attractions got to know each other through their favourite records. It soon became clear there wasn't much common ground, apart from the go-to's – The Beatles, The Rolling Stones and Small Faces – while the others were amused to find that Steve Nieve's rock'n'roll appreciation extended only to Alice Cooper and T. Rex. Regardless, The Rolling Stones' *Aftermath* was the one album that got the nod from everyone, and it became a regular in Elvis' rotation while writing material for *This Year's Model*.

This almost-title-track drew its inspiration directly from 'Stupid Girl': a sneering takedown that didn't do The Stones many favours in appealing to the fairer sex. Later calling it an 'answer song' to 'Stupid Girl', Elvis later explained that his words were meant to come from a place of disappointment instead of disgust, but that didn't stop contemporary reviewers from labelling him a misogynist. 'In any case', he shrugged, 'most of these songs were works of imagination rather than products of experience'.

'The Beat' (Elvis Costello)

Elvis and The Attractions slow things down with 'The Beat': a soulful celebration of sexual freedom and the eventual frustration of interruption. Unwelcome authority figures run rampant throughout ('Vigilantes coming out to follow me', ''Til a man comes along and he says/Have you been a good boy, never played with your toy?/Though you never enjoy such a pleasure to employ'), while sexual innuendo and allegations abound ('Anybody wanna swallow me?', 'It takes two to tumble, it takes two to tango/Speak up, don't mumble if you're in the combo'). The final verse finds the narrator talking from personal experience, almost as if delivering a cover letter on a résumé ('Oh, I don't want to disease you/But I'm no good with machinery', 'I don't go out much late at night/I don't go out much at all').

'Pump It Up' (Elvis Costello)

A-side, 28 April 1978; Peak position: 24.

During the month-long Live Stiffs tour in the autumn of 1977, legions of sycophants, hangers-on, groupies and pushers, latched onto the bands – Nick Lowe, Wreckless Eric, Ian Dury and The Blockheads, Larry Wallis, and Elvis and The Attractions – and it was here that the real excess began: '(it) started pretty much from when there was any money about, or from the first time people realised it was a happening band', Bruce Thomas later recalled. 'Once people realise that, people appear from everywhere offering you this and that. Nothing succeeds like perceived success.'

Elvis had largely avoided the illicit substances and extramarital affairs up to this point, but he gave into temptation soon enough. A constant presence in dressing rooms and on the tour bus was a mysterious woman known as Farrah Fuck-it-Minor (a reference to Farrah Fawcett-Majors), who would become Steve Nieve's companion for many years and mother of his two children. However, her loose connection to the keyboardist didn't prevent her from straying to other band members, and she had affairs with both Bruce Thomas and Elvis, both of whom fell hard for her.

Ashamed by his immediate downfall from family man to tawdry womaniser, Elvis penned a lengthy screed, 'scrawled on the fire stairs of a Newcastle hotel in an amphetamine and vodka frenzy. The sex-and-drugs-and-rock'n'roll life beckoned, amply demonstrated both day and night during the infamous Live Stiffs package tour. This anti-rock'n'roll song was my last stand before I gave in to it completely. The painful morning brought a large but simple editing job, allowing us to learn to play the song the next evening in Lancaster'.

Thus, 'Pump It Up' was born, and in its finished recorded version (laid down five days after being written, and in only one take) is a tenacious rant, spit out a mile-a-minute. Just as Bob Dylan's 'Subterranean Homesick Blues' had been an answer song to Chuck Berry's 'Too Much Monkey Business', so too was 'Pump It Up' to Dylan's broadside, though the subject matter was more personal: here, instead of ranting about mundane annoyances or championing the counterculture movement, Elvis took a look at himself in the mirror, hated what he saw, and wrote it down. 'Well, just how much can you fuck? How many drugs can you do before you get so numb you can't really feel anything?'

Released in April 1978 as the second single from *This Year's Model,* 'Pump It Up' (backed with 'Big Tears') peaked at number 26 in the UK.

'Little Triggers' (Elvis Costello)

According to Elvis, 'Little Triggers' is the 'ballad of *This Year's Model*', and while the song wears its influences – country soul mixed with the pop sheen of Burt Bacharach – on its sleeve, he acknowledged a third, perhaps more surprising influence: the backing vocals of Iggy Pop's 'Turn Blue', from *Lust for Life*. 'You can tell there's a sort of change of mind', he explained, 'change of attitude, I suppose. Whereas 'Alison' went on to be covered by Linda Ronstadt and a bunch of other people, and was sort of my calling card song (I suppose, in some people's views, it still *is* one of my best-known songs), 'Little Triggers' … is a different animal completely. A darker song'.

'You Belong to Me' (Elvis Costello)

B-side of '(I Don't Want to Go To) Chelsea', 3 March 1978.

Following the release of *This Year's Model*, Elvis was accused of rampant misogyny in many of his lyrics – a charge which surprised him – explaining that he often wrote more from the viewpoint of disappointment than condemnation. It comes as little surprise that 'You Belong To Me' was one of the main offenders, from its dominating title to the lyrical theme of submission. As ever, context is key: The Rolling Stones' *Aftermath* (itself rife with many seemingly anti-women songs) was in heavy rotation on the tour bus during Elvis and The Attractions' first US tour. While Elvis later acknowledged the parallels between 'This Year's Girl' and 'Stupid Girl', he didn't mention that 'You Belong To Me' borrows the introduction from 'The Last Time', or the nod to 'Under My Thumb' ('You act dumb, you say you're so numb/You say you don't come under his thumb'), or the outro's bass glissando reminiscent of '19th Nervous Breakdown'.

'Hand In Hand' (Elvis Costello)

'I never really understood the accusations of misogyny that were levelled at the lyrics on *This Year's Model*', Elvis later shrugged. 'They clearly contained more sense of disappointment than disgust. In any case, most of these songs were works of imagination rather than products of experience. The temptations and distractions of the touring life would soon enough add the more cynical and guilty edge found in 'Little Triggers', 'Pump It Up', and 'Hand In Hand'.'

Right from its opening line – 'No, don't ask me to apologise/I won't ask you to forgive me' – Elvis is on the defensive, dancing between sneering malice ('If I'm gonna go down/You're gonna come with me') and feigned innocence ('Don't you know I got the bully boys out/Changing someone's facial design'). The threats are more comically thuggish and empty than they are intimidating, and even Elvis isn't convinced: 'But you can't show me any kind of hell/That I don't know already'. As he would later discover, he was his own worst enemy.

'(I Don't Want To Go To) Chelsea' (Elvis Costello)

A-side, 3 March 1978; Peak position: 16.

When The Attractions were formed in the summer of 1977, Elvis made it clear that he was the songwriter and they were his band. It may have been a little hard-nosed, but he had a clear vision of how he wanted his songs to be recorded, and, with none of the other musicians being particularly adept at songwriting, he was the one who was in charge of coming up with the goods. However, Elvis wasn't ignorant to the obvious strengths of The Attractions and was willing to entertain suggestions that might benefit the song.'(I Don't Want To Go To) Chelsea' was originally written as a slower acoustic rocker, yet with the same stop/start guitar figure as The Who's 'I Can't Explain' or The Clash's 'Clash City Rockers'. This arrangement was fleshed out in rehearsals for The Attractions' debut concerts and was attempted in the studio, but The Attractions had some tweaks: 'Bruce and Pete came up with a more syncopated rhythm pattern and Steve found a part that sounded like sirens – although he rarely played the same thing twice, so you had to pay attention'.

Elvis took aim at the fashion-forward Chelsea district, a west London neighbourhood famous for being the centre point of Swinging London in the 1960s. A decade later, Vivienne Westwood opened her 'Sex' boutique and her boyfriend, Malcolm MacLaren established his headquarters in Chelsea; he would quickly make something of Johnny Rotten and Sid Vicious. ''Ha bloody ha' said the first taxi driver that I asked to take me there after the record came out', Elvis later wrote.

He also devoted a few pages to his feelings on Chelsea – in his autobiography, *Unfaithful Music and Disappearing Ink* – and the impression it made on him during a rare father/son outing at the tail end of the 1960s. 'Now,' he lamented in his 1977 self, 'Chelsea seemed even more of an unattainable neighbourhood. It stood both for the groovy past and was reported in the papers as the hotbed of the new punk ferment; apparently, the work of dastardly haberdashers or people who had half grasped some French political manifesto from 1969'. Or, as *Rolling Stone* critic, Kit Rachlis, so wonderfully put it, 'Costello can describe Chelsea with such precision because he knows its splendours. If the disdain in his voice appears a little too measured, it's because it takes all of the singer's resolve to resist Chelsea's temptations'.

Released as the first single from *This Year's Model*, '(I Don't Want To Go To) Chelsea' followed 'Watching The Detectives' into the top 20, peaking at 16. (The song was omitted from US editions of the album, as was 'Night Rally', for being 'too British', though both songs were released as a stand-alone single in Canada.) Elvis was later amazed at how quickly his success had skyrocketed: 'When I wrote the song, I was living in the suburbs with my wife and young son, one false move away from penury. By the time the song was issued as The Attractions' first single release, we were already on our second record label, had made two circuits of the British club and concert circuit, toured America for the first time, got banned from US television, and completed *This Year's Model* in just eleven days, either side of Christmas 1977'.

'Lip Service' (Elvis Costello)

Another nod to The Rolling Stones and their rollicking pop/rock album, *Aftermath*, 'Lip Service' finds Elvis at his punning best, with lip service equaling both oral sex ('Don't make any sudden movements/These are dangerous amusements') and bored, disconnected agreement. However, he draws heavily from mid-period Beatles for the arrangement, with ringing acoustic guitars, a melodic bass line from Bruce Thomas, and a chiming piano melody from Steve Nieve.

Interestingly, the main chorus phrase ('Lip service is all you'll ever get from me') was purloined from his earlier composition, 'Cheap Reward', which had been written and recorded in late 1975 and premiered on Charlie Gillett's BBC Radio London programme, *Honky Tonk*.

'Living In Paradise' (Elvis Costello)

Written while Elvis was still in Flip City, 'Living In Paradise' was given a run-through at the band's recording session at Hope and Anchor Studios in early 1975. Even this embryonic version has most of the lyrics in place, though a few lines had yet to be finalised, namely the original opener, 'Every day I see a rich man in a poor man's disguise', which was changed to the more sinister and possessive, 'I don't like those other guys looking at your curves'.

When Elvis turned professional, he deliberately left much of his Flip City repertoire in the past, though he felt that 'Living In Paradise' was worth dusting off for the *My Aim Is True* sessions. Taken at a quicker clip, this arrangement veered perhaps too heavily towards C&W than Stiff Records would have liked, and the song was discarded from consideration. Only with the eventual rewrite and an arrangement influenced by his new band, would Elvis deem 'Living In Paradise' finally worthy of release.

'Lipstick Vogue' (Elvis Costello)

Apart from the requisite feeling-each-other-out period of their early shows, The Attractions had proven themselves to be a live force to be reckoned with (what's interesting is that, even when Elvis' opinion of The Attractions was at its lowest, he always gave high praise for their musical prowess). Recognising the need to capture the urgency and immediacy of a band at their peak, Nick Lowe ushered Elvis and The Attractions into the studios over an 11-day period to get the absolute best performances out of them for *This Year's Model*. While the entire album is a testament to both band and producer, on 'Lipstick Vogue' especially, there's no way that Lowe would have been able to coax the perfect blend of runaway cacophony and tight precision had The Attractions not been as road-tested as they were. (By this point, they had performed just over 50 concerts in less than four months.) As stunning as the studio take is, check out any live version from The Attractions' peak period for a glimpse of how awesome they truly were.

'Night Rally' (Elvis Costello)

The final song on *This Year's Model* offers a chilling glimpse of the present, written as a response to the unnerving rise in neo-Nazis, supported by nationalists and the likes of Eric Clapton, who had gone on a drunken onstage racist rant that directly led to the formation of Rock Against Racism. (Of course, Elvis would have his own drunken racist rant the following year, but we'll get there.)

'Night Rally' castigates naivety and ignorance, with the narrator well aware of what the National Front is doing: rounding up dissenters or those who never thought fascism could ever actually happen again. Set to a military-style rhythm, with Pete Thomas' drum pattern equaling the marching feet of millions of imaginary fascists lining up for the rally, the song throws brainwashing, paranoia, and totalitarianism into the mix. Steve Nieve's keyboard sound is positively sinister, no more so than on the extended coda, where he mimics the sound of an air raid siren while drums and cymbals crash and the bass swoops and dives before unexpectedly ending mid-word.

Related Tracks

'Big Tears' (Elvis Costello)

B-side of 'Pump It Up', 28 April 1978.

Elvis has held much affection for the sole outcast from the *This Year's Model* sessions, even wondering why he omitted it from the final running order. Perhaps it has to do with the more graphic nature of the lyrics – inspired by the 1968 film, *Targets* – based on the real-life random killing spree by Charles Whitman two years prior. Or perhaps it was the apparent disapproval from certain Attractions, at the presence of Clash guitarist Mick Jones, who guested on this and an unreleased take of 'Pump It Up'. Whatever the reason, one of Elvis and The Attractions' finest performances (even notorious grump Bruce Thomas has consistently cited this as one of his favourite Costello compositions) was relegated to B-side status, appearing as the flipside of 'Pump It Up'.

'Radio, Radio' (Elvis Costello)

A-side, 20 October 1978; Peak position: 29.

When Elvis and The Attractions were about to hit the road in the summer of 1977, he took some of his older Flip City songs and dusted them off for a revival. One of those songs was 'Radio Soul', originally written as a lighthearted shuffle that celebrated the golden age of radio. But Elvis' opinion of radio had soured in the intervening three years. He also found himself victim to the stodgier side of the music industry, though he often disguised his passive-aggressive confrontations as naïve innocence (regarding the *Saturday Night Live* incident: 'I believed that we were just acting in the spirit of the third word of the show's title, but it was quickly apparent that the producer did not agree'), and his more aggressive battle with the music press was notorious and would soon prove a disastrous tactic.

Recognising that his success could come crashing down at any moment, Elvis went all-out with 'Radio, Radio', changing its tone from one of sympathy to one of sabotage.

I want to bite the hand that feeds me
I want to bite that hand so badly
I want to make them wish they'd never seen me

As he sang elsewhere on *This Year's Model:* 'If I'm gonna go down/You're gonna come with me'.

Surprisingly, 'Radio, Radio' didn't sink him, though DJs were reluctant to spin a song so critical of their format: this perhaps accounted for its mediocre placing of number 29 in the UK. Columbia Records didn't seem to care about the song's message, nor its *Saturday Night Live* notoriety, and included it on *This Year's Model* at the expense of '(I Don't Want To Go To) Chelsea' and 'Night Rally'.

Funnily enough, art would imitate life: former BBC Radio One disc jockey, Tony Blackburn – whose bubbly yet canned personality made him moderately likeable (though he stubbornly refused to play songs by progressive, punk, and new wave bands) – called Elvis a 'silly little man' on air. As dictates the laws of coincidence and bad timing, Blackburn was the host of *Top Of The Pops* the following week, which featured none other than Elvis and The Attractions performing 'Radio, Radio'. Elvis, not one to forgive and forget, amended the line 'such a lot of fools' to 'silly little men' and shook an angry fist at Blackburn off-camera.

'Tiny Steps' (Elvis Costello)

B-side of 'Radio, Radio', 20 October 1978.

After assessing the songs he had written for what would become *Armed Forces* during The Attractions' lengthy spring 1978 US tour, Elvis was disappointed in discovering that he had essentially rewritten *This Year's Model*. While some songs would be salvaged, others like 'Talking In The Dark', 'Wednesday Week', and 'Tiny Steps' were deemed surplus to requirements and were snuck out on various single releases.

'If ('Tiny Steps') sounds like it belongs on *This Year's Model*, then it was probably for the benefit of the documentary film crew who were climbing up the walls and crawling across the floor in an attempt to capture us in an act of recording our 'new sound'', Elvis later explained, somewhat obliquely. 'For reasons I cannot explain, we elected to sound as much like our last record as possible.'

'Crawling To The U.S.A.' (Elvis Costello)

Released on *Americathon* soundtrack, 1979.

The 1979 film, *Americathon* – set in the future (1998, to be exact) and depicting a nation that has run completely out of oil – was a forgettable satire though with an impressive cast featuring John Ritter and Fred Willard, with cameo appearances by Jay Leno, Meat Loaf, and a certain Elvis Costello, portrayed in the film as the Earl of Manchester. Apart from allowing '(I Don't

Want To Go To) Chelsea' to appear on the soundtrack, Elvis and The Attractions contributed an original composition – 'Crawling to the U.S.A.' – which, like the film, is forgettable, if not enjoyable. The song was recorded during their first Australian tour in December 1978 at Waterloo Studios in Sydney. Apart from the film's soundtrack album, the song also featured on Elvis' compilation albums *Ten Bloody Marys And Ten How's Your Fathers* and *Taking Liberties*.

Armed Forces (1979)

Personnel:
Elvis Costello: vocals, guitar
Steve Nieve: keyboards
Pete Thomas: drums
Bruce Thomas: bass guitar
Recorded at Eden Studios, London, August–September 1978
Produced by Nick Lowe
UK release date: 5 January 1979; US release date: January 1979
Highest chart places: UK: 2, US: 10
Running time: 36:26

The release of *This Year's Model* and its three UK Top 30 singles necessitated a veritable whirlwind of almost instantaneous promotional activity by Elvis and The Attractions. Over 120 shows were performed between January and late July 1978 – a gruelling schedule for even the most seasoned band – so it's no surprise that a luxurious three-month break (apart from a handful of local radio and TV appearances) was embraced so warmly. However, the break wasn't all rest and relaxation: Elvis, ever the prolific writer, had a stockpile of songs that he debuted at various concerts throughout the year, and the plan was to enter Eden Studios once again to commit the songs to tape. 'Sunday's Best' was the 'oldest' of the bunch, having been written and performed in October 1977, while most of the other new material would be road-tested and fleshed-out in front of frantic audiences.

Even some of the other band members were starting to write their own songs: Steve Nieve composed three songs that Elvis felt were worthy of being performed onstage alongside his own material. Two of these – 'Arms Race' and 'Damage' – were never seriously considered as album songs, though the third song, 'Sad About Girls', was recorded during sessions for *Trust* in the autumn of 1980, by which time all three of Steve's songs had been released on The Attractions' debut 'solo' album, *Mad About the Wrong Boy*.

For now, though, Elvis had plenty of material that he wanted to record. His writing had also started to take on a more sinister tone: in addition to the relationship failures explored on *My Aim Is True* and *This Year's Model*, he also expanded upon the totalitarian scenarios painted in 'Night Rally'. How much of this was Elvis' doing compared to his manager (Jake Riviera) manipulating him has been up for debate; Riviera always made sure that Elvis played up the hostility card, not to only audiences but also the press. This put the critics in a precarious situation: while reviewing the albums and shows, their praise was almost universal, but they couldn't get a civil word from Elvis. An embargo on interviews was implemented, partly due to Elvis' disinterest in playing the public relations game and partly to Riviera's combative nature. Reports of the road crew assaulting local press for photographing Elvis were not uncommon at this time. Things would go from bad to worse within a year.

There was also a tender side to Elvis – while on tour in California in June 1978, he became enamoured with Bebe Buell: a well-known model/groupie who had been romantically linked to, among others, Todd Rundgren and Steven Tyler from Aerosmith, with whom she had a daughter, Liv. Elvis and Buell immediately hit it off, and a sordid affair that would dog Elvis' emotions and songwriting for the next six years started in earnest; yet, in the self-penned liner notes for the 2002 *Armed Forces* CD reissue, he unequivocally denied that any of the songs on the album were written about her, despite claims (including her own) to the contrary:

> On the eve of recording this album, a girl arrived on my doorstep from America. At best, we were strangers with a coy and theoretical entanglement. I thought that she might be coming for a short visit and that I might at least satisfy my curiosity about her. However, she turned up with eight pieces of luggage like a mail-order bride and moved in. I was too stupid and vain to resist. She'd later claim to have inspired most of the songs on this record – all of which were already written when we met. This was also said about the previous release – a chronological impossibility – and many other of my compositions to this day. It is a tragic delusion about which I wish I could say, 'I shall not dignify that with a response', but 'dignity' doesn't come into this story.

Sessions for *Armed Forces* (known first as *Cornered On Plastic* and then *Emotional Fascism*) began in earnest in the late summer of 1978, with Elvis and The Attractions cutting nearly twenty songs for inclusion. Six weeks were afforded the recording – a luxury by their standard – which accounts for its bright sheen and skilful production. Like many Elvis albums, it's timeless, though not of its time, and this is down to the team of Nick Lowe and Roger Bechirian, who had come so far by this time that they were able to tailor the sound to Elvis' ever-growing musical demands. However, the songs were also important, and Elvis drew musical inspiration from various unlikely sources. Instead of reproducing the mid-1960s sound that inspired *This Year's Model*, Elvis had been listening to artists like David Bowie (his highly experimental *Station to Station*, *Low*, and *Heroes* albums were constants for Elvis' on the road), Kraftwerk, Iggy Pop, and The Beatles' experimental era, though it was the unexpected inspiration of ABBA that would give Elvis and The Attractions their biggest hit.

The album was released in January 1979, preceded by 'Oliver's Army', which became a huge hit single and helped escalate *Armed Forces* to number 2 in the UK and 10 in the US. Wrapped in a delightfully garish Barney Bubbles cover looking like an artist's paint supply had exploded over a canvas (the UK cover was altered to a herd of elephants stampeding through a boneyard), the album received some of the highest praise of Elvis' entire career, with hardly a negative review in sight.

But all that goodwill was put in a precarious position when Elvis and The Attractions started their highly controversial Armed Funk tour; by the end of it, Elvis would be the most reviled man in the rock world (at least for that week). The mood was set early on by manager Jake Riviera, who took the heavy-handed lyricism of *Armed Forces* to the extreme by spray-painting 'Destination: Camp Lejeune, NC' on the sides of the tour bus, and reminded tour manager Des Brown to not allow any reporters or photographers to come anywhere near Elvis. As Riviera himself later said, 'The trouble is that when you say to journalists that my artist is too talented to talk to you – instead of talking to you and the *Columbus Gazette*, he could be writing a song, which is more important in the great scheme of things – they don't like it. In fact, they hate it'.

To paraphrase Elvis' then-current US single, the situation was an accident waiting to happen, and it took the night of 15 March 1979 for things to unravel. After a fairly perfunctory gig at the Agora Club in Columbus, Ohio, Elvis, The Attractions and their entourage returned to the nearby Holiday Inn to discover another tour bus had shown up. 'I remember seeing this other bus in the driveway of the hotel and the general feeling on our bus was, 'Another group! Right!'', Pete Thomas recalled in a March 1992 *BBC Radio One* documentary. 'It would be like if sailors had come into harbour and found another boat there, and they knew they were having a night off. 'Oh, we're bound to end up having a punch-up with them'. And then finding out who it was. Whoooah! It's Stephen Stills! The old school.'

Stills, of course, had been alternately one-third or one-fourth of the biggest American country-rock band in the 1970s – Crosby, Stills & Nash (and occasionally Young, depending on his mood) – but he was also the founder of Buffalo Springfield and a respected solo artist in his own right. However, he was known for being particularly difficult to work with and, by 1979, Stills was an anachronism: old, washed-up, and irrelevant. That he was presently touring with former Delaney & Bonnie vocalist, Bonnie Bramlett, only confirmed to the new wave how out of touch with things he was; not to mention his challenged cocaine habit, which Elvis later playfully – if hypocritically – poked fun at by calling him 'Old Tin Nose'.

With The Attractions still riding various highs, the entourage discovered their to-be sparring partners sitting in the bar of the Holiday Inn, enjoying a drink and each others' company. Pete and Steve didn't stay too long, preferring to get a good night's sleep over chatting with Stills and Bramlett, but Elvis clearly had other things on his mind. The conversation started off innocently enough, with Elvis and Bruce alternating between feigned interest and good-natured ribbing, but quickly devolved into deliberate egging-on. The two Brits apparently had something of a schtick, where they would shout loudly at Americans that they were only here to steal their music, their money, and their women, and this grated against Stills and Bramlett. When a fan witnessing the melee asked Elvis what he thought about Americans, he upped the ante: 'We hate you. We just come here for the money. We're the original white boys, and you're the colonials'. He then called America a nation of 'flea-bitten greasers', which only set Stills off: he picked Elvis up by his lapels, shook him around a bit and stormed out.

Bramlett herself was getting worked up and accused Elvis of stealing from R&B and Tamla Motown music, to which Elvis retorted that James Brown was nothing but a 'jive-ass n****r' and Ray Charles a 'blind, ignorant n****r'. The now-infuriated Bramlett responded by taking a swing at Elvis but only succeeded in pushing him off his stool, dislocating his shoulder in the process. As he crawled up to his room, he left Bruce in the middle of the fracas, resulting in a great deal of pushing and shoving from the assembled entourage.

The downfall was swift. Bramlett sold her story to the press, which in turn prompted Elvis to respond, 'I was completely drunk, and I tried to outrage them by racist remarks, trying to shock them by criticising people so beyond criticism. Unfortunately, Americans do not share my irony. My words were way off, no excuse. They had the desired effect: to start a fight. I didn't think anything more about it, and certain members of that entourage took it upon themselves to inform the American liberal press that I was a cover racist, and we were in deep trouble.' Far less contritely, he seethed that Bramlett had 'made one reputation off of one EC (Eric Clapton), and she's fucking well not going to get more publicity off another one'.

But she did. As soon as the story broke, *Armed Forces* – which hit the American top 10 only the day after the incident – plunged quickly in the charts. Then, Rock Against Racism – a campaign set up in 1976 as a response to the then-threat of racial conflict and white nationalism – began picketing Elvis' concerts. (Never mind that Elvis had appeared at a free gig in support of the move six months earlier.) The damage had been done, but Bruce alleges that this might have been partly intentional on Elvis' part: 'We never really recovered from that tour. Every time Elvis is doing something well, he kind of sabotages it. Even then, that mechanism was at work, subconsciously sabotaging the possibility of being a really big A-league band. We were probably poised to be like Elton John or Bruce Springsteen'.

In order to placate the media, Elvis and Jake Riviera went into damage-control mode, holding a press conference on 30 March at CBS Records' Manhattan offices. Anyone who was in such a situation would have appeared truly contrite, maybe shifting a well-placed tear or two and appealing for mercy at the feet of the media. But this being Elvis Costello, grovelling was not on the agenda, and while the press conference started off well enough, soon the media began to shout questions at him, not exactly about the incident, but about how they had been handled by Riviera's goon squad. It seemed that their bottled-up frustrations over being denied access to Elvis, were finally spilling out.

While he explained his actions, he neither made excuses nor apologised to Stills and Bramlett: 'As I'm not a racist, why do I have to apologise?'. He then made the mistake of claiming his words had been taken out of context. Richard Goldstein from *The Village Voice* (incidentally, the paper that had first broken the news and called Elvis a racist) angrily shouted back, 'You weren't available for comment! I tried for hours to reach you. You made yourself unavailable! Don't blame it on the press. It's not the press; it's you! You said it and you were unavailable to clarify it'.

The press conference probably did more harm than good at first. Relations between artist and media remained tense at best for the next few years, though many would begrudgingly offer top marks to subsequent album releases. Considering the number of death threats Elvis received as a result of the incident, two armed bodyguards were needed to assist him in New York City. Even CBS Records lost interest in promoting the new album and briefly considered dropping him from their roster. Instead, they let him dangle, and when Riviera suggested that they book Shea Stadium on the strength of 250,000 requests for a draw of free Elvis tickets on the radio, the label declined. In typical Riviera fashion, he had a truckload of shovels delivered to their headquarters, with a terse note attached: 'If you really want to bury my act, I thought you could do with some help'.

While the controversy has been largely forgotten, Elvis, for his part, still hasn't forgiven himself for his actions, devoting an entire chapter to the incident in his autobiography, *Unfaithful Music and Disappearing Ink*:

> Didn't they know the love I had for James Brown and Ray Charles, whose recording of 'The Danger Zone' I preferred to watching men walk on the moon?' 'My love for the world is like always'. How could you not know that? It seems that they did not. It took just five minutes to detach my tongue from my mind and my life from the rail it was on. Does anything else that I've done in the other 59 years and 525,550 minutes suggest that I harbour suppressed racist beliefs?

Elvis seemed to agree with Bruce Thomas' assertion that the incident was an act of self-sabotage. Perhaps when he saw the wreck that Stephen Stills had become, Elvis saw a similar (or worse) fate for himself; he later acknowledged that 'that Ohio evening may very well have saved my sorry life. I fear an obituary might have appeared not too much later, just a few short lines lamenting my unfulfilled promise on the occasion of a tawdry demise. When I say this, I do not refer to the many anonymous people who offered to shoot me, but to the emptiness that I was already feeling and my ferocious pursuit of oblivion. So what if my career was rolled back off the launching pad? Life eventually became a lot more interesting due to this failure to get into some undeserved and potentially fatal orbit'.

In the liner notes to the 2003 CD reissue of *Get Happy!!*, Elvis recounted (with the benefit of diplomacy and nearly 20 years of hindsight) the events that transpired that evening, before adding a touching postscript:

> I was standing backstage at a gala show in Los Angeles with a group of friends in the dingy, concrete loading bay, when I saw a man in dark sunglasses being led in our direction. It was Ray Charles, and as he drew level, his assistant stopped to introduce him to the singer at my side. Realising that to try and offer any apology after all these years would do little more than embarrass everyone present, all I could do was turn my head away with shame and frustration, knowing that this was a hand that I will probably never shake.

He never did: the legendary musician died on 10 June 2004.

Let's give the final word to Ray Charles then, for he showed not only understanding and compassion for Elvis but harboured no ill will: 'Anyone could get drunk at least once in his life. Drunken talk isn't meant to be printed in the paper, and people should judge Mr. Costello by his songs rather than his stupid bar talk'.

'Accidents Will Happen' (Elvis Costello)

A-side, 4 May 1979; Peak position: 28.

There is a distinct difference in the lyric matter on *Armed Forces*: songs that have nightmarish, Orwellian story lines, and songs that were based on events in Elvis's personal life. The most telling is 'Accidents Will Happen': an obvious candidate for the best-disguised admission of guilt that Elvis has ever written. Though he hadn't yet embarked on his marriage-destroying affair with Bebe Buell, Elvis had succumbed to the wild infidelities of rock-star life while on tour, and though it disgusted him (hence his lengthy rant, 'Pump It Up'), he wasn't about to give it up. He later called the song a 'heartless apology and barely-coded confession'; a simple switch of person from third to first ('he' becoming 'I') confirms this.

Continuing the tradition of heralding an album *a cappella*, 'Accidents Will Happen' was an obvious choice as opener, replacing 'Clean Money' at the last minute. Nick Lowe's production is more grandiose, with an air that is an appreciated reprieve from the terse production of *This Year's Model*. The instrument that carries the melody here is the bass (as opposed to the guitar, which is almost nonexistent; if it is present, it's buried deep in the mix), while Steve Nieve creates a good atmosphere with his assortment of keyboards. This is a fine ensemble performance, and 'Accidents Will Happen' has rightly been considered one of Elvis and The Attractions' most mature arrangements to date.

In a great bit of unfortunate irony, the song was chosen as the follow-up single to 'Oliver's Army', though it came hot on the heels of the Columbus incident. Released in May 1979 and backed with 'Talking In The Dark' and 'Wednesday Week', the single faltered at 28 in the UK: by no means a disappointment, but considering that 'Oliver's Army' had catapulted Elvis and The Attractions to 2 in their homeland, this fall from grace was swift and merciless. Elvis would later dryly note, 'For a brief, improbable moment, the horrified children of Britain were offered magazines featuring pop pin-ups of myself and the most handsome band in the world, right alongside Debbie Harry and those other blonde beauties, The Police. Thankfully for all concerned, I was just about to screw it all up completely'. The aptly-titled single did little to appease both an indifferent public and a legion of increasingly angry music journalists, who had, up to this point, begrudgingly praised Elvis' albums but were turned off by his arrogance and unwillingness to play the public relations game.

Elvis has retained an affection for the song, performing it live nearly 1,000 times between 1978 and 2020, though its only live appearance to be released to date was recorded at the Hollywood High School, where it was drastically rearranged and used to open the setlist. Featuring only Elvis on vocal and Steve Nieve on grand piano, the song takes on a more sombre tone, and it's evident that, even at this early stage, Elvis was flirting with the idea of escaping the pop rock mentality for which *Armed Forces* was championed; this new arrangement sounds closer to 'Shot With His Own Gun' and 'Just A Memory' than the album's finely-crafted pure pop production, and would serve in Elvis recognising Steve's remarkable talent as a pianist.

'Senior Service' (Elvis Costello)

This is a public put-down of office politics and the callousness of cut-throat business – in this case, quite literally ('Because there's always another man/ To chop off your head and watch it roll into the basket'). Set to a herky-jerky, deceptively rhythmic yet undanceable arrangement, 'Senior Service' is a production delight, with layers of vocal harmonies and cutting-edge technology (Steve Nieve employed the use of a Jupiter-8 synthesizer, most noticeable in the bridge); take a bow, Nick Lowe.

As for the title, this is a rare triple-entendre: the most obvious is seniority; less obvious to non-Britons is that Senior Service is more formally known as the Royal Navy (and is thus the first reference to the 'armed forces'); and perhaps the most oblique reference is to a British-specific brand of cigarettes. 'It's a breath you took too late/It's a death that's worse than fate' indeed.

'Oliver's Army' (Elvis Costello)

A-side, 2 February 1979; Peak position: 2.

Who knew that a song about Oliver Cromwell's life in the 17th century would give Elvis and The Attractions their biggest hit single ever in the UK? Certainly not Elvis, who originally considered it a throwaway B-side until Steve Nieve added the perfect ingredient: a piano part that referenced ABBA's massive hit single, 'Dancing Queen'. With this new addition, Elvis could no longer argue that 'Oliver's Army' wasn't worthy of single release – a smart decision on his part, for it went on to reach number two in the UK in February 1979 and catapulted him and The Attractions to pop stardom for a few weeks.

Depending on who's telling the story, Cromwell is either a regicidal dictator or a heroic leader; very few would consider him to be the latter. In 1649, he led an invasion of Ireland that was fuelled mostly by religious and political hatred toward the Roman Catholic church. The result was the banishment of Catholicism and around 12,000 Irish people being sold into slavery under the newly established Commonwealth of England. All of this has very little to do with the song itself; according to Elvis, the origin came upon his 'first trip to Belfast in 1978 and saw mere boys walking around in battle dress with automatic weapons. They were no longer just on the evening news. These snapshot experiences exploded into visions of mercenaries and imperial armies marauding around the world. The song was based on the premise, 'they always get a working-class boy to do the killing'. I don't know who said that; maybe it was me, but it seems true nonetheless'.

Elvis' Catholic upbringing influenced his vision of Cromwell, admitting to *Time Out* that he had been portrayed as 'the devil incarnate'. Furthermore, Elvis' paternal grandfather, Patrick Matthew McManus (sic), had been shot and injured in action in France during the Great War and recuperated at Beggar's Bush Barracks in Dublin. Costello biographer, Graeme Thomson, put it best in his book, *Complicated Shadows,* that 'it's a supreme irony that the grandfather of the author of 'Oliver's Army' – that deceptively jaunty indictment of the English military's brutalisation of Ireland – didn't return to the Front upon his recovery, but instead found himself as a non-combative soldier in the British Army in Ireland at the time of the rising Republican tide in 1916'.

The song started life as a tentative piano-and-voice number, which Elvis and Steve performed live, shortly after it was written, on 16 April 1978 at the Roundhouse; by the time the band arrived in Denmark for the Roskilde Festival on 2 July, it had become a full band arrangement, though Elvis still considered it a throwaway B-side. 'I wasn't particularly aware that that was going to be our anthemic song', Bruce Thomas later remembered. 'Some of them I thought were pretty good songs, like 'Big Tears', were never big songs. It's hard to tell.'

Once the song made it to the studio, Steve transformed it – somewhat innocently and unintentionally – from a 'Don't Worry, Baby' pastiche to the grand, sweeping production piece it became. 'Nick and I were like, 'This is a fucking hit!'' engineer Roger Bechirian later recalled. 'You could smell it from the first note. They were cutting the basic track intro and we were just in hysterics, thinking this is just so good. We couldn't wait to get it finished.'

Elvis and The Attractions quickly discovered that the fame and attention that came from having a number two single in the charts would work against their best interests, though that was in the long run; the immediate effect was that the audience changed from devoted fans to screaming teenagers. 'I saw people responding without any kind of understanding or consideration', Elvis later complained. 'We'd play a set where we'd play brilliantly all night and then we'd do our hit single and people would go crazy. Yet they would be bewildered by the rest of what we were doing.' Yes, the single sold nearly 500,000 copies, and Elvis and The Attractions were finally getting noticed, but Elvis didn't want to be a pop star – he wanted to be a musician, and the irony that a song about British militarism was his biggest single in the UK, didn't escape him: 'You could sing along with the chorus without ever thinking what it was about'.

'Big Boys' (Elvis Costello)

With its muscular backing – due in no small part to the recent introduction of synthesizers to Steve Nieve's already large array of keyboards – 'Big Boys' chugs along tenaciously with Pete's drums and Bruce's distorted bass mixed well to the fore. The story is one of thuggery, goonery, and romantic justice dressed up in violent language; considering Elvis' own promiscuity on the road by this point, it's not too much of a leap to conclude that he's transmitting his confessional in coded language. Bruce Thomas later succinctly noted, 'Either (Elvis) doesn't want anyone to know what he's talking about, or he doesn't know what he's talking about himself'.

'Green Shirt' (Elvis Costello)

A-side, 4 May 1985; Peak position: 68.

Elvis marvelled at the vastness of North America on his and The Attractions' first tour, later noting that while navigating the nation's highways and byways in a crammed station wagon, 'every shop front or nightclub sign seemed like a line from a song. In some cases, that was just what they became. Wasn't there likely to be something dastardly going on at any place called the Quisling Clinic? It was just up the road from our hotel'.

The Quisling Clinic, located in Madison, Wisconsin, was a prewar medical building founded by relatives of Vidkun Quisling: a Norwegian politician who assisted Nazi Germany in overthrowing his country's government so that he could take power. (Because of this, the term 'quisling' is now slang for 'traitor' or 'collaborationist'.) Despite its fairly mundane status as a medical treatment centre, Elvis conjured up horrible goings-on in the Quisling Clinic, associating it with a story about political backstabbing ('She's picking out names, I hope none of them are mine') reminiscent of blacklisting and McCarthyism of the 1940s and 1950s.

The story begins with the narrator watching the news one evening, only to discover the ensuing scandal that he may or may not be involved in. The 'smart young woman on a light blue screen' is none other than Angela Rippon, erroneously credited as being the first female newscaster in the UK (that honour belongs to Barbara Mandell, who landed a job on ITV in 1955), though she was the first female newscaster to hold the job for an extended period, having joined the BBC in 1974, hosted the 1977 Eurovision Song Contest and *Top Gear*, and reported coverage of Prince Charles and Princess Diana's wedding in July 1981.

'Green Shirt' is one of those songs that has invited interpretation and discussion since its release, yet Elvis has always been reluctant to discuss it at length. Even the ever-informative CD notes skimmed over the subject matter, with Elvis talking more of the musical construction than the lyrical subject. What is for certain is that the song is one of his most lyrically bleak and paranoid, which he admits was fuelled by 'late hours and my chemical constitution (which) were exaggerating the creeping threat, but the coincidences added the surreal edge into the sensory overload and the paranoid tone of (the song)'. Married to a light and breezy musical backing with Steve Nieve providing the baroque melody (sounding like a harpsichord, it was actually played on a Jupiter-8 synthesizer, while the pulsating rhythm throughout the song was created and looped on a Minimoog synthesizer), the song is punctuated by close-mic'ed blasts of drums and heavily-distorted bass, while Elvis is nearly drowned out by the noise as his half-whispered vocals tell the story. It's not quite the film noir and creepy reggae of 'Watching The Detectives', but it's just as sinister.

Overlooked for single release at the time, 'Green Shirt' was released in May 1985 to help promote the compilation *The Man (The Best of Elvis Costello)*. The standard 7' vinyl had 'Beyond Belief' as the B-side, while the 12' vinyl release added an extended remix by Colin Fairley, that, to be quite frank – and in common with some other remixes specific to the format – is not really worth seeking out.

'Party Girl' (Elvis Costello)

The requisite torch song isn't so much a ballad as it is a slower rock song, with plenty of melodic guitar and a fine-tuned Attractions arrangement. Elvis later wrote that 'Party Girl' was, 'written for an art student that I barely knew. I found our meeting reported in the tatty gossip of a Midwestern newspaper. I was handed the improbable role of 'rock star', and certain assumptions were made about the character of the girl in the title. Some small kindness and tenderness passed between us; I could do no more than resent the portrayal and offer this apology. The song is not so much 'hopelessly romantic' as simultaneously romantic and without hope'.

'Goon Squad' (Elvis Costello)

One of the darkest and most foreboding songs written by Elvis to date, 'Goon Squad' is the chilling tale of an innocent and wide-eyed teenager sent off to a military training camp, marvelling at the possibilities ('They said they'd make me major if I met all their demands'), but along the way becomes brainwashed into a hardened, thoughtless goon.

Whatever the song's true meaning may have been, was obscured by Elvis' fascination with wordplay and innuendo, leaving the listener to just assume the worst, given the title; then again, it could very well be about a young professional entering the workplace ('I could be a corporal into corporal punishment/Or the general manager of a large establishment'). But context is the key; remember that Elvis and his manager, Jake Riviera, were feeding off of each other's paranoia around this time and that the Armed Funk tour would become Elvis and The Attractions' most confrontational. Riviera hired henchmen to handle and 'take care of' intrusive journalists, overzealous fans, sneaky bootleggers, and innocent photographers at concerts. He would even insist that the road crew wear army fatigues and decorated the tour bus with a block-lettered sign, 'Destination: Camp Lejeune, NC' (home of the US Marine Corps).

Driven by a distorted bass and rolling drum pattern – with Steve Nieve's siren-like keyboards wailing away – 'Goon Squad' is the perfect culmination of Elvis' overindulgence in drugs and the tireless efforts of a road-weary Attractions (also consumed by the same indulgences), with the tense atmosphere creating a flawless composition and performance.

'Busy Bodies' (Elvis Costello)

Sounding like a cast-off from *This Year's Model*, 'Busy Bodies' 'contains the densest and most neurotic juggling of words in order to simply state that promiscuity wears you out', Elvis later explained. As ever, he uses puns to get his message across ('Now you're ready for the merger with the company you're part of/And you do the dirty business with your latest sleeping partner'), though they're a bit forced when compared to his other songs of sexual discovery.

Elvis was later critical of 'Busy Bodies', stating that 'Tiny Steps' probably should have replaced it in the final running order. Regardless, the song is, as Elvis later reasoned, redeemed by 'a very ambitious vocal line and a guitar figure related to Roy Orbison's 'Oh, Pretty Woman'', and it's hard to disagree with him there. It may not be as immediately catchy as 'Oliver's Army' or 'Accidents Will Happen', but it still has its merits, namely the gorgeous vocal harmonies toward the conclusion.

'Sunday's Best' (Elvis Costello)

Set to a bizarre circus ground waltz, 'Sunday's Best' was 'another song that contained thoughts of class and notion', Elvis later wrote, while noting that it was 'originally written for Ian Dury, or at least in something approaching his style. The bewildered, xenophobic narrator was the kind of pathetic character that might have invited some pity in Ian's hands. It was also another song constructed out of shop signs and newspaper slogans'.

The song was written on 31 October 1977 during the Live Stiffs tour, when Wreckless Eric spotted the line, 'Stylish slacks to suit your pocket', in a newspaper advertisement and made an offhand mention of it to Elvis. Elvis, who was prone to fits of inspiration and competition at unlikely moments, turned to Eric and said, 'Let's have a race to see who can get it into a song first'. Of course, Elvis won – though whether Eric actually tried to write a song with the line or just humoured Elvis is unknown – and premiered the song to a bemused Eric later that day on the tour bus, playing it live that night.

'Moods For Moderns' (Elvis Costello)

Perhaps the least substantial track on *Armed Forces*, 'Moods for Moderns' sounds like Elvis and The Attractions fused with Booker T & the M.G.'s and David Bowie's 'Berlin' albums. Sure, you can dance to it, but there's not much here in terms of lyrics: with the odd structure of two half verses combined with the title repeated eight times, one full verse and a bridge, all repeated again for good measure, Elvis doesn't say a whole lot.

'Chemistry Class' (Elvis Costello)

On the surface, 'Chemistry Class' combines the lyrical themes of lust and references to the Holocaust ('Are you ready for the final solution?'), though there's a deeper meaning to Elvis' words. The 'chemistry' in the song refers to the mutual attractions of a relationship, with Elvis desiring more than a one night stand (the first part of the chorus is clever: Elvis sings, 'You've got a chemistry class/I want a piece of your – mind'), though the 'final solution' is the more mundane parting of ways when the relationship ultimately deteriorates. The final verse ties in nicely with the album's opening song, 'Accidents Will Happen': 'If it wasn't for some accidents, then some would never ever learn', with an intentional skip added over 'accidents'.

Elvis later explained that the song 'was a reaction to the complacence of some of the university campuses that we visited on those first trips to America. As a teenager, I'd grown up reading magazine articles about radical student politics in the '60s. At times we seemed only to encounter uncomprehending hedonism or braying superficiality. I could only imagine such people sliding blithely into some repressive future. Either that or they might find an excellent career in advertising. I wasn't feeling very reasoned in my arguments'.

'Two Little Hitlers' (Elvis Costello)

The year before the release of *Armed Forces*, Nick Lowe issued a single titled 'Little Hitler', also released on his *Jesus of Cool/Pure Pop For Now People* album. (Incidentally, *Little Hitler* was the working title for *This Year's Model*, though more rational heads prevailed.) That same year, Elvis wrote a song called 'Two Little Hitlers' that, apart from having a somewhat similar title, had little else in common with Lowe's song; Elvis's 'was about a loveless egotistical couple. It paints an unflattering picture of the whole courtship dance. The bridge makes a passing reference to a speech from Charlie Chaplin's *The Great Dictator* ('He's an unnatural man'), but other than that had nothing to do with 20th-century history. Musically, I think the clicking guitar part came from listening to early Talking Heads records'.

Fascism is indeed nowhere to be found in the story; Adolf Hitler is only used as a reference to the arguing couple, who 'fight it out until/One little Hitler does the other one's will'. Considering Elvis' marital discord around this time, it's more than likely he was referring to himself and his increasingly estranged wife, Mary.

Complete with some fairly lame wordplay ('She so calculating/She's got a calculator') and a narrative that just goes on and on and on, the song is a marginal conclusion to what has been regarded as one of Elvis and The Attraction's best albums. (The fade-out repetition of 'I will not burn/I will return' was probably more of a cry of defiance than being relevant to the story and took on an ironic tone in light of the Columbus incident.) Thankfully, for anyone who purchased the US edition, they still had '(What's So Funny 'Bout) Peace, Love and Understanding?' to get to.

Related Tracks

'(What's So Funny 'Bout) Peace, Love and Understanding?' (Nick Lowe)

B-side of Nick Lowe's 'American Squirm', 23 November 1978.

The free love movement of the 1960s culminated in the three-day Woodstock Festival of August 1969, one of the most celebrated declarations of peace, love, and understanding, which also happened to include some of the greatest rock musicians of the 20th century. That movement – and the late-1960s as an ideal – ended less than six months later at Altamont Speedway, where the Rolling Stones hired members of the Hells Angels (on the recommendation of the Grateful Dead and Jefferson Airplane) to serve as security. Pumped up with adrenaline and free beer, the Hells Angels turned what should have been a peaceful concert into one of carnage.

Not only that, but some of the pioneers of the rock world – Jim Morrison, Brian Jones, Janis Joplin and Jimi Hendrix – were either dead or would die soon. The early-1970s stumbled and faltered as new bands came and went; glam rock was a passing phase, which eventually begat arena rock and disco, while punk rock and new wave were the obvious solutions to bloated corporate rock.

In the middle of all this musical change, Nick Lowe wrote a song called '(What's So Funny 'Bout) Peace, Love And Understanding?', released as the opening track of pub rockers Brinsley Schwarz' 1974 album, *The New Favourites of Brinsley Schwarz*. Elvis, an unabashed Brinsley Schwarz fan, was immediately taken with the song and incorporated it into his setlists while on tour with The Attractions in the summer of 1978. While recording *Armed Forces* in August of that year, Lowe was also working on material for his follow-up to *Jesus of Cool*: *Labour of Lust*. 'American Squirm' was released as the lead single from the album and featured Elvis on backing vocals and the Attractions rhythm section. The B-side was a studio recording of '(What's So Funny 'Bout) Peace, Love And Understanding?', performed by Elvis and The Attractions but credited to Nick Lowe and His Sound.

Elvis later explained that Lowe had his tongue planted firmly in his cheek while writing the song and that people merely misinterpreted the song's seemingly pacifist message as something more serious than it actually was. Listening to Elvis' version, it's hard not to see the song as anything more than a plea for a more caring world, though the vocal delivery is more forceful (peace by compulsion). Regardless, the song was immediately accessible and successful, with Elvis and band banging away with little restraint, turning the song into a powerful anthem, which explains why the original intent was lost on many listeners. Elvis' voice here is more serious and believable, disposing of any humour that may have been ingrained in the words. The Attractions, too, play as if their lives depend on it, and the end result is energetic and breathless.

Unsurprisingly, the song has won many plaudits over the years from fans and critics alike, citing it as one of the quintessential Attractions songs and an instance when a cover version surpassed the original. Elvis has held much affection for the song, performing it at nearly every concert since 1978: almost 1,400 times. Though its only commercial single release was as the B-side of Lowe's 'American Squirm' single in November 1978, the song was issued as a giveaway single (with 'My Funny Valentine' as the B-side) on Valentine's Day 1979 at Elvis and The Attractions' Long Beach Arena show. More mundanely, Columbia apparently decided that 'Sunday's Best' was 'too British' for American audiences, instead replacing it with this song, tacking it onto the end of *Armed Forces*.

'Talking In The Dark' (Elvis Costello)

A-side, 18 December 1978; Peak position: did not chart. Also released as the B-side of 'Accidents Will Happen', 4 May 1979.

Elvis later claimed this song as 'a modest but heartfelt song to a confidante of mine, written in the exhausted hours when lust requires only sympathy'. While it's easy to understand why 'Tiny Steps' was excluded from the final running order of *Armed Forces*, it's surprising that 'Talking In The Dark' couldn't have been shoehorned in, especially considering its brevity (less than two minutes). Perhaps the lyrics didn't convey a suitable mood, though the story of a man driven insane without the companionship of his latest flame seems to be consistent with most of the lyrics on *Armed Forces*.

With a synthesizer solo plucked straight from 'Maxwell's Silver Hammer', 'Talking In The Dark' makes its point and moves on. The song – along with its B-side 'Wednesday Week' – would, in December 1978, become the first new single release from the *Armed Forces* sessions, but didn't count as a conventional release: only 9,000 copies were pressed, with all given away for free at Elvis' Christmas shows at the Dominion, three New York shows the following month and with a purchase of the new album at any UK concert throughout January. Still recognising both songs' strengths and not wanting them to be forgotten, Elvis insisted on the pairing being released as the double B-side of 'Accidents Will Happen' in May 1979.

'Wednesday Week' (Elvis Costello)

B-side of 'Talking In The Dark', 18 December 1978, and 'Accidents Will Happen', 4 May 1979.

Sounding like two songs rolled into one, the first half of 'Wednesday Week' moves along at a speed that threatens to fall apart at any given moment: The Attractions thrash away while Elvis howls through the words incomprehensibly, while the second half slows down to something resembling an amalgamation of 'Accidents Will Happen' and 'Oliver's Army', and finally he is able to be understood, singing, 'You took the words out of my mouth/And put your tongue into my cheek/But I'd better lose my memory by Wednesday week'. Elvis called the song 'a chillier item; a two-part trifle in which insincere lovers put each other on something rotten. The second part of the song is the most obvious of our affection for the Wings singles that we always seemed to find on truck-stop jukeboxes'.

Bonus Ep: 'Live At Hollywood High'

Included as a complimentary extra with *Armed Forces*, this three-track live EP was recorded at Hollywood High School on 4 June 1978 and features 'Accidents Will Happen' and 'Alison' on one side, and an extended 'Watching The Detectives' on the B-side. (Track one is deliberately misspelt as 'Adcidents Will Happen'.) These three tracks were later released on the 1993 Rykodisc reissue of *Armed Forces*, while six additional tracks appeared on the album's 2002 double-disc reissue. The full show was finally released in 2010 and is well worth seeking out.

'My Funny Valentine' (Richard Rodgers, Lorenz Hart)

B-side of 'Oliver's Army', 2 February 1979; Also released as a free 7' Valentine's Day giveaway with '(What's So Funny 'Bout) Peace, Love And Understanding', 14 February 79.

Perhaps one of the most unexpected covers that Elvis performed this early in his career, 'My Funny Valentine' was the first instance of him recording (and later releasing) a solo session, though this would continue regularly throughout his tenure with The Attractions. Elvis later said that it was 'a song that I had known since I was a child. I don't know what prompted me to record it; maybe someone was late for the session and I was just filling time. It was an oddly romantic choice in the circumstances. I just had lousy judgment in such affairs'. Of course, he is talking of his disintegrating marriage to his wife Mary and the tumultuous beginnings of an affair with Bebe Buell.

With music by Richard Rodgers and lyrics by Lorenz Hart, the song has been performed by over 600 artists and is a jazz standard. Written in 1939 for the musical comedy, *Babes In Arms* and first sung by Mitzi Green, it was undoubtedly Chet Baker's 1952 recording that attracted Elvis' attention. 'My Funny Valentine' was later pressed – with '(What's So Funny 'Bout) Peace, Love And Understanding?' – as a free red vinyl single for a show at Long Beach Arena on Valentine's Day 1979. (Fun fact: in 2011, my girlfriend at the time, who's now my wife, acquired a copy of this giveaway single for our first Valentine's Day together. I think I got her a gift card to Olive Garden which we used that night.)

Get Happy!! (1980)

Personnel:
Elvis Costello: vocals, guitar; organ on 'Possession'; all instruments on 'New Amsterdam'
Steve Nieve: piano, organ
Pete Thomas: drums
Bruce Thomas: bass guitar; harmonica on 'I Stand Accused'
Recorded at Wisseloord Studios, Hilversum, Netherlands, and Eden Studios, London, October 1979.
Produced by Nick Lowe, except 'New Amsterdam' by Elvis Costello.
UK release date: 15 February 1980; US release date: February 1980.
Highest chart places: UK: 2, US: 11
Running time: 48:21

Elvis and The Attractions' fourth full-length album release in just under four years, was written following the Columbus incident, though only two of the songs on the final album ('Black And White World' and 'Riot Act') made any reference to this controversy, and even then, obliquely. The rest of the material was influenced by Elvis' extramarital affairs: around this time, The Attractions' touring schedule was so intense that he was hardly at home, and his marriage to his wife Mary was falling apart. Though the two would attempt reconciliations over the next few years, the one woman for whom Elvis fell hardest – Bebe Buell: an American model who had dated, among others, Todd Rundgren, Rod Stewart, Jimmy Page, and Aerosmith's Steven Tyler – continued to pop up throughout this period. The temptation was too hard to resist, and Elvis found himself drawn into a tempestuous and fractured relationship.

Elvis maintained that the stylistic shift from the tight pop/rock of *Armed Forces* to the overstuffed, shambolic *Get Happy!!* – with many arrangements either directly lifting from or subtly referencing old Stax and Motown records – wasn't calculated, telling *Record Collector's* Peter Doggett in September 1995:

> It just happened that I was listening to a lot of the music I'd loved when I was 15 – a lot of Motown and Stax and Atlantic. I was digging out singles and trying to find odd tracks that had funny sounds on, for inspiration, really. We literally made the decision to start again over a couple of pints of beer. We'd had a couple of days in the studio where we tried to play those arrangements, but they'd sounded wretched, so we went to the pub and said, 'What are we gonna do? Why don't we all try playing some of these songs slower and use more rhythmic accompaniment, rather than these tricky, nervy kind of backing that we'd been using?' And it just fell into place.

Always a prolific songwriter, Elvis brought a truckload of new songs to the sessions in October 1979. The decision to record abroad – at Wisseloord Studios in Holland – was not by choice but by necessity in order to instil some new freshness into the songs already written. Unfortunately, the lures of nearby Amsterdam often meant that sessions were unintentionally sabotaged, while the band's hectic itinerary afforded them no time to relax and recover. 'By that time, we were pretty far gone on Peruvian hay fever powder (cocaine), and the rest of it', Bruce Thomas later admitted. 'Pete and I used to stay up for nights on end, and we'd turn up to the studio kind of ... just gone.'

Pete Thomas would later say that the sessions were 'all to do with the Nick Lowe school of Most Possible Excitement In the Studio, which can obviously only be taken to a certain level sober. You know, with an early night's sleep. And then gets a lot more interesting —if more erratic – once you introduce 'substances' and things to drink'. The drummer also claimed that Bruce started seeing beetles crawling around the studio floor, while Elvis admitted that 'everything was played too fast because of our attitude at the time. It wasn't in control. It was very maniacal and emotional. But somewhere in the heart of the better songs is some sort of purity. I garbled the words and bellowed. Sometimes I was overbearing. Sometimes I got right to the point, (while) other times I blew straight past it'.

It's hard to disagree with him. The beauty of *Get Happy!!* isn't in the intricacies or subtle nuances of the songs because there aren't any. It's the way that Nick Lowe's production captures a band ready to break off the leash, with each member furiously attacking his instrument: four members leading the band in different directions. The record is deranged and frantic, manic and impenetrable, convoluted and bloated, making it the exact opposite of Elvis' previous albums, all of which had been pristinely recorded and presented so that every instrument and lyric could be discerned and deciphered. On *Get Happy!!*, everything is thrown together, from the error-ridden back sleeve (which has the two sides of the record reversed, so that 'I Can't Stand Up For Falling Down' begins it and 'High Fidelity' ends it, though the vinyl was presented correctly) to the slapdash front sleeve, which features a bright orange backing with large blue font loudly proclaiming the album title and band, obscuring three faded and similar images of Elvis, placed haphazardly on the sleeve. A wear ring is imprinted into the sleeve to make it look like a well-loved compilation album from the 1960s.

For the first time, the band had recorded enough material for a double album, but instead of whittling down the cream of the crop for another tight 12-track album, Elvis and Nick Lowe crammed ten songs each onto both sides of the plastic, with a running time nearing 50 minutes. While the band could have easily released a double album (six additional tracks and one remake of an existing song were also recorded, eventually slipping out as contemporary B-sides), this would have defeated the *modus operandi* of *Get Happy!!*; Elvis wanted to put out something as claustrophobic and bewildering as possible. The critics agreed as they praised it: *NME* said, 'Elvis and The Attractions have pared their sound right down to the bone. There are no solos, no synthesizers, and almost no overdubs ... There's a much better rhythm and expression here'; while *Melody Maker* opined, 'Twenty-track avalanches are difficult to absorb – tracks that first seemed weak have now come up smiling, and others may follow…'.

'Love For Tender' (Elvis Costello)

A brief and straight-to-the-point introduction to *Get Happy!!*, 'Love For Tender' shatters any pretence that the album will be a natural successor to *Armed Forces*: a dense fog of layered organs, gated drums, muddled vocals, and a bass line carrying the melody toward the upper register of Bruce's fretboard, the song is a confusing, glorious mess that finishes just as it gets going. Musically recalling The Supremes' 'You Can't Hurry Love', the title is a sly pun on the other Elvis' 1956 hit, 'Love Me Tender', though the song was originally recorded during sessions for *Armed Forces*, as the claustrophobic 'Clean Money'.

'Opportunity' (Elvis Costello)

After the frantic opener of 'Love For Tender', the pace is slowed down considerably with 'Opportunity', one of the few songs on *Get Happy!!* to reach over three minutes. The song is driven by Steve and Bruce as Elvis croons of a paranoiac's conspiracy theory of surveillance and being followed: 'They shop around, follow you without a sound/Whatever you do now, don't turn around'.

'The Imposter' (Elvis Costello)

In his liner notes to the 2003 double-disc reissue of *Get Happy!!*, Elvis called 'The Imposter' one of the slighter songs from the album, though made special mention of the middle eight ('When I said that I was lying/I might have been lying'), coyly mentioning that it wasn't coincidental that the follow-up album was titled *Trust*. The song itself is a rollicking roller-coaster of a ride, barely hanging on for dear life as The Attractions come close to falling apart. Despite its slightness as a song, 'The Imposter' embodies the roller-coaster-ride spirit of *Get Happy!!* perfectly in its brief duration, making it one of the more enjoyable recordings on the album.

'Secondary Modern' (Elvis Costello)

Another snippet of a song, running just under two minutes, 'Secondary Modern' was, like 'Opportunity', Elvis and The Attractions' attempt to play like Al Green's backing band, though Elvis later admitted there was little to suggest their intentions in the finished arrangement. Regardless, 'Secondary Modern' is set to the slow burn of a soul groove, with Steve's Hammond organ working overtime. The lyrics, however, are more ambiguous, possibly making a reference to innocence lost ('Is it out of the question between you and me?/Is it pleasure or business or a packet of three?'), while the lines, 'Nobody makes me sad like you/Now my whole world goes from blue to blue', sound endearingly naïve from a man who has written weightier lines.

'King Horse' (Elvis Costello)
With its lyrics borrowed from an earlier, unpublished Elvis composition, and a guitar figure borrowed from The Four Tops' 'Reach Out (I'll Be There)', 'King Horse' is a superb song, dripping with swaggering machismo that hides 'the kind of vain and foolish fellow I feared that I might have easily become'. The song taps into an in-progress bar flirtation between a woman cloaked in 'cheap cut satin and bad perfume' and a man who'd 'seen the bottom of a lot of glasses/But he'd never seen love so near'. The flirtatious dance goes on, and just as he pleads to consummate his passion with her, she pulls away, out of his life, and he returns to his beer and the jukebox.

'Possession' (Elvis Costello)
Opening with a nod to The Beatles' 'From Me To You' ('If there's anything that you want/If there's anything that you need'), 'Possession' – an ode to money and the evil it brings with it – was written 'in a Dutch taxi during a five-minute journey back to the studio after I had become drunkenly besotted with the waitress in a local café. The song was cut the same evening with the singer propped up behind the Hammond organ'. As ever, the narrator is vengeful, singing to an ungrateful lover ('You lack lust, you're so lacklustre/Is that all the strength that you can muster?'), and the venom in the lyric is underscored by a fairly impassioned, but hardly violent, vocal delivery – when he sings the title, Elvis sounds more wearied than angry.

'Men Called Uncle' (Elvis Costello)
With its title recalling the 1960s US TV series, *The Man From U.N.C.L.E.*, 'Men Called Uncle' starts off as a lambasting of younger women going after older men before turning into genuine sympathy. After a night of passion with the woman, the narrator finds that he has affection for her and wishes she would cease her destructive lifestyle. 'As you check your effects and check your reflection/I'm so affected in the face of your affection'.

'Clowntime Is Over' (Elvis Costello)
A song of lament and regret, 'Clowntime Is Over' is set to a wall of ringing acoustic guitars and heavily-echoed drums, with Steve Nieve's Hammond organ the most prominent instrument. Despite its curious lyrics, it is a fine composition.

'New Amsterdam' (Elvis Costello)
Solo A-side, 7 June 1980; Peak position: 36.
Elvis explained that this was 'a song about a bewildered new arrival in the New World'. But more importantly, this is the first truly solo Elvis recording to be issued since he signed a record deal. It had proven impossible for the band to improve upon the earlier demo, which featured Elvis on all instruments (in addition to the prominent, ringing acoustic guitar throughout, he also

played electric guitar, bass, and Hammond organ) and had been recorded at Archipelago Studios: a £15-an-hour facility in Pimlico, London.

It's fairly common knowledge that New York City had been known, until 1664, as New Amsterdam; hence, lines such as 'Back in London they'll take you to heart after a little while/Though I look right at home I still feel like an exile', are astoundingly poignant. The overwhelmed outsider is determined to be like 'the transparent people who live on the other side/Living a life that is almost like suicide'. More profoundly, the song reads as an update of 'Stranger In The House': with his extramarital affairs now well-publicised, a contrite Elvis had returned home, cap in hand, to attempt to smooth his marriage over.

'High Fidelity' (Elvis Costello)

A-side, 4 April 1980; Peak position: 30.

With the first line of the song borrowed from The Supremes' 'Some Things You Never Get Used To', 'High Fidelity' is a charging, driving rocker, propelled by a pummelling bass line and melodic piano, while Elvis reaches new lows in the vocal register department, almost crooning along and sounding like he's barely breaking a sweat. This high-energy rocker tackles the subject of infidelity, a topic very close to Elvis' heart around this time. However, while the subject matter is drawn from events in his life, 'High Fidelity' is not autobiographical or confessional. Instead, it takes the viewpoint of a jaded protagonist, undoubtedly stalking the true object of his affection ('Even though you're nowhere near me/And I know you kiss him so sincerely now'), while trying to convince himself that he's happy enough with his current relationship status ('Lovers laughing in their amateur hour/Holding hands in the corridors of power/Even though I'm with somebody else right now').

The song was released in April 1980 as the follow-up single to 'I Can't Stand Up For Falling Down', but didn't reach the same heights of success. Backed with a cover of Van McCoy's 'Getting Mighty Crowded' (additionally, the UK 12' disc also contained a remake of 'Clowntime Is Over'), the single struggled to number 30 in the UK: The Attractions' poorest chart position since their formation.

'I Can't Stand Up For Falling Down' (Homer Banks, Alan Jones)

A-side, 18 January 1980; Peak position: 4.

While Elvis had adapted several obscure cover versions in live shows, the appearance of 'I Can't Stand Up For Falling Down' marked the first time he released a cover on an album. Kicking off the second side of *Get Happy!!* with an infectious riff, the song was transformed from a slowed-down and soulful Sam & Dave B-side into a rocker bursting with frenetic energy and exuberance. Presumably, the stacks of Stax singles that Elvis has mentioned as the influence on the sound of *Get Happy!!*, must have included the 1967 vinyl release of 'Soothe Me': instead of using that song as an influence on an original Costello number, the band merely reworked it as their own.

'Black And White World' (Elvis Costello)
Considering the recent media outburst against Elvis following the Columbus incident, it's not surprising that the singer would address such issues in his then-recent songs. What is surprising is that he didn't address it further than 'Black And White World' and 'Riot Act', both times mostly indirectly.

The former song takes a look at the media, though there's no hostility or bitterness about how he had been portrayed. Instead, there's a sense of nostalgia, a longing for how things used to be: 'When I was just a boy and men were men'; while reference to last year's model is made: 'Those days she was just a beautiful girl/Now she's framed and hung up'.

'5ive Gears In Reverse' (Elvis Costello)
Get Happy!! is a particularly bass-heavy album, with Bruce Thomas allowed creative freedom on this standout track from the second side. His bass work throughout the song is exemplary, meshing wonderfully with Elvis' jangly rhythm guitar and Pete's steady drumming. The title itself, deliberately spelt with the number 5 instead of the letter F, seems to imply that, instead of progressing as a society, we are regressing in new and creative ways.

But if your patience is exhausted and you still cannot decide
You're sitting in the garage contemplating suicide
And you have no motivation you can't even catch your breath
All of this acceleration is driving you to death

'B Movie' (Elvis Costello)
With passing references to domestic abuse ('You can't stand it when I throw punchlines you can feel', 'It's not your heart I want to break'), 'B Movie' equates a girl of whom Elvis is less than fond, with a cheap flick ('B movie, that's all you are to me/Just a soft soap story/Don't want the woman to adore me'), wishing to discard her in a fashion similar to how moviegoers quickly forget less-than-stellar films.

'Motel Matches' (Elvis Costello)
Written as a country song but slowed down to a heartfelt ballad, 'Motel Matches' weaves an intriguing story. The narrator finds himself in an unsatisfactory relationship ('Though you say I'm unkind/I'm being as nice as I can'), and through the paper-thin walls of his motel, can hear the goings-on around him: television, night-time noises ('Boys everywhere fumbling with the catches'), and even Wanda Jackson's 1961 song, 'Who Shot Sam?'. The man equates his affair to the casual passing of a matchbook from one person to another, though the apathy is reciprocated: 'Though your mind is full of love/In your eyes there is a vacancy'.

'Human Touch' (Elvis Costello)

Influenced by Elvis' recent work with The Specials (he had produced their eponymous debut album just before sessions for *Get Happy!!*), 'Human Touch' is a plea from a romantically stifled man for compassion and companionship. Alternately, it could hint at some form of physical abuse (the narrator gloats of his victim that he'd 'like to fix her in a picture of rage'), which would be explored more in-depth in the next song.

'Beaten To The Punch' (Elvis Costello)

This song was perhaps the most direct reference to Elvis' affair with Bebe Buell that he would make on record – and even then, 'Beaten To The Punch' was twisted and distorted to conceal the truth. Elvis learned this tactic from a Picasso biography he had been reading at the time and was especially tickled to learn that the artist implemented secret codes and messages in his works, specifically to his lovers. Figuring that a good idea is worth exploring once, Elvis left breadcrumbs of encoded and cryptic language throughout *Get Happy!!*, for his bit on the side: specifically, 'Motel Matches', 'Men Called Uncle', 'Riot Act', and this Merseybeats-inspired noisemaker.

'Temptation' (Elvis Costello)

In the liner notes to the 1989 compilation, *Girls Girls Girls,* Elvis wrote of 'Temptation', that the song 'started out as a holier-than-thou snipe at a 'very famous rock star', who I imagined to be breathing his own artificial atmosphere. However, by the time we came to record it, I'd had a good lungful of the same poison but had also located that slippery addictive feeling that you get just before giving in to something wicked'. Based on Booker T. & the M.G.'s 'Time Is Tight', the song slinks along nicely, with Bruce and Steve duelling for attention, while Elvis very nearly howls the words, crying the final line – 'Give me temptation' – as if it were his mantra.

'I Stand Accused' (Tony Colton, Ray Smith)

Originally recorded and released by The Merseybeats in 1965, The Attractions' recording of this cover sounds more like a glorious deconstruction than a faithful play-by-the-numbers rendition. Though 'I Can't Stand Up For Falling Down' would rightly receive more attention, 'I Stand Accused' is no slouch either, somehow bottling the band's raw energy into a two-and-a-half-minute onslaught of pent-up aggression and anger. The Attractions zoom through the song while sounding unhinged, about to fly off the track at any second. Bruce Thomas is the instrumental star of the show, with an exceptionally busy bass line leading the melody while he howls into a harmonica toward the song's end. Meanwhile, Elvis sings like a man possessed, making no attempt to constrain his voice or prevent it from cracking, helping add to the feebleness of trying to prove his innocence when he's already been branded guilty.

'Riot Act' (Elvis Costello)

The Columbus incident had affected Elvis deeply, and the stress of the situation – as well as general dissent within the band – forced him to reevaluate his worth as a musician. Unsurprisingly, he had come to the conclusion that he would be better off quitting the music business completely, and 'Riot Act' was his sign-off. Opening with the lines 'Forever doesn't mean forever anymore/I said forever/But it doesn't look like I'm gonna be around much anymore', the song details his brush with ignorant drunk-talk ('Why do you talk such stupid nonsense/When my mind could rest much easier/Instead of all this dumb, dumb insolence/I would be happier with amnesia') and the immediate regret it caused. With a hard-working Steve Nieve on piano and organ, the song chugs along in a slow burn, with a heavily-echoed Pete thudding his drums while Bruce solos beneath Elvis. This is a quintessential Attractions recording, and they never sounded this good before or since. If this had been their swan song, it would have been only too perfect.

Related Tracks

'So Young' (Joe Camilleri, Jeff Burstin, and Tony Faehse)

Elvis and The Attractions recorded this 1978 Jo Jo Zep and The Falcons track with the intent of issuing a summer 1979 single. Elvis and band entered Abbey Road Studios on 28 May 1979, and he later noted that the 'session fell on a bank holiday and was blighted by flying coffee cups, technical resistance, and overwhelming blueness'. Perhaps this explains why the production credit intimates that it was recorded 'at gunpoint by Nick Lowe'. While the song is enjoyable enough – with an exemplary instrumental track – it's hard to imagine it being a hit single. Nor would it have been welcome on *Get Happy!!*, being of medium tempo and having none of the manic claustrophobia of any of the other songs. Besides, two covers were enough. 'So Young' never materialised as a single and was left unreleased until the *Out of Our Idiot* compilation in 1987.

'Girls Talk' (Elvis Costello)

B-side of 'I Can't Stand Up For Falling Down', 18 January 1980.

Written by Elvis and then, in a drunken act of charity, given away to Rockpile (much to manager Jake Riviera's anger) – who would have a massive UK hit with it, reaching number 4 in October 1979 – 'Girls Talk' as recorded by Elvis and The Attractions has been labelled as one of their great lost classics, though it would be hard to imagine the song on *Get Happy!!*. Indeed, the first version – which is dominated more by bass than any other instrument – was perhaps a bit too slow to fit among the more raucous moments of the album, though its brevity would have been ideal for the album. (A later second version sounds more like a drunken attempt to mash the lyrics with 'Pump It Up': needless to say, it doesn't work well at all.) In this version, it sounds more like 'Opportunity' or 'Secondary Modern', and would have been a neat companion piece to those songs. Nevertheless, it was this version that was issued as the B-side of 'I Can't Stand Up For Falling Down', which, incidentally, achieved the same success as Dave Edmunds' version of 'Girls Talk'.

'Getting Mighty Crowded' (Van McCoy)

B-side of 'High Fidelity', 4 April 1980.

Another song issued as the B-side of 'High Fidelity' in April 1980, 'Getting Mighty Crowded' – itself a cover originally recorded by Betty Everett – was recorded for *Get Happy!!* but ultimately left off the album, presumably because it was decided that two covers were enough. The song is particularly enjoyable, with a great ensemble performance and some particularly amusing falsetto backing vocals by Elvis. Apart from being released as a B-side, 'Getting Mighty Crowded' was later issued on the *Taking Liberties* and *Ten Bloody Marys & Ten Hows Your Fathers* compilations in 1980.

'Clowntime Is Over No. 2' (Elvis Costello)

B-side of 'High Fidelity', 4 April 1980.

Issued as the B-side of 'High Fidelity' in April 1980, this slower version of 'Clowntime Is Over' was drastically different from the recording that appeared on *Get Happy!!*: slowing down the tempo to an almost dirge-like pace, dominated by an ethereal Hammond organ and Elvis' strained voice. Evidently, the band were displeased with this first recording, and the familiar remake was recorded, thus making the album version, in effect, No. 2.

'Dr. Luther's Assistant' (Elvis Costello)

B-side of 'New Amsterdam', 7 June 1980.

Elvis later recalled this song being written in 1977 and briefly considered for inclusion on *This Year's Model*, though it went unrecorded by The Attractions. They did, however, perform it live briefly – during a two-month span between October and December 1977 – before it was discarded and not heard from again. For whatever reason, Elvis brought the song out of mothballs in March 1980 and recorded a new demo, playing all of the instruments, before Pete Thomas overdubbed the drums at a later date. Modelled after the more psychedelic leanings of The Byrds and The Move, the lyric was inspired by a fantasy Elvis once had about a disused local cinema, presumably involving a psychotic doctor's assistant. It's easy to see why the song was passed over, and it would certainly have been out of place on Elvis' sophomore album.

'Ghost Train' (Elvis Costello)

B-side of 'New Amsterdam', 7 June 1980.

Recorded at the same session as 'Dr. Luther's Assistant' in March 1980, 'Ghost Train' was adapted from an earlier song titled 'Maureen and Sam', which had been written with school friend and Rusty bandmate Allan Mayes. Why Elvis was going through his past songwriting repertoire and committing these early compositions to tape is anyone's guess, but 'Ghost Train' is a curious recording, featuring the singer on all instruments, including amateurish fretless bass and comical marimba. Elvis explained that the song had been rewritten in 1976 and 'fictionalised some of the cabaret turns that I saw in Northern England clubs when going to see my father perform in the early 1970s', and that Mayes still performed the song in live performances. (In fact, Mayes released the original version on his 1986 album, *Stumbling In the Aisle*.) As for Elvis's version, it appeared on the largely solo EP release of 'New Amsterdam', along with 'Dr. Luther's Assistant' and 'Just A Memory'.

'Just A Memory' (Elvis Costello)

B-side of 'New Amsterdam', 7 June 1980.

Recorded at T.W. Studios in Fulham, with Elvis on vocals and Steve on keyboards, 'Just A Memory' was written as an imitation of Burt Bacharach, with an ideal vocalist of Dusty Springfield. It's likely that this performance was meant as a demo for Springfield, though it did end up on the *New Amsterdam* EP in June 1980. The song is taken at a slow, almost grandiose pace, with particularly beautiful vocals from Elvis, occasionally drifting off into falsetto for extra texture. Simply sublime.

'At the time, I had no idea or little confidence about how I might contact (Dusty)', Elvis later recalled. 'However, several years later, Dusty's producers must have recognised the intention of the song (now re-titled 'Losing You'), as it was recorded for her album, *White Heat*, with the inclusion of a specially-written second verse that brought it closer to a conventional length composition.' This verse, which was apparently 'sung down a transatlantic telephone line', would later be incorporated into live performances.

Trust (1981)

Personnel:
Elvis Costello: vocals, guitar; all instruments on 'Big Sister's Clothes'
Steve Nieve: piano, organ
Pete Thomas: drums
Bruce Thomas: bass guitar
Additional personnel on 'From a Whisper to a Scream':
Glenn Tilbrook: vocals
Martin Belmont: guitar
Recorded at Eden Studios, London, October-November 1980.
Produced by Nick Lowe (not to blame for 'Big Sister's Clothes'), in association with Roger Bechirian.
UK release date: January 1981; US release date: January 1981
Peak positions: UK: 9, US: 28
Running time: 41:53

As the aftermath of the Columbus incident started to die down, Elvis and The Attractions designed their strategy for the new decade. Elvis had been writing prolifically during this period; even his faithful Attractions had been steadily accumulating a collection of songs, most notably from Steve Nieve, who must have felt some degree of frustration at not being able to contribute his own material. During a break in the touring schedule, The Attractions – minus Elvis, but plus guitarist, Tim Renwick – were ushered into Eden Studios to record their debut 'solo' album, *Mad About the Wrong Boy* (later sarcastically dubbed *Too Clever By Two-Thirds* by Elvis), which failed to gain much interest apart from a cursory listen by the most curious Costello completists.

Not all was rosy with the tortured frontman: as he later wrote, 'My self-induced fatigue had convinced me to take the melodramatic decision to quit show business'. Finding himself slipping deeper and deeper into alcohol and substance abuse, and with his marriage in tatters because of the constant presence of Bebe Buell, Elvis was well on his way to becoming a casualty of the rock and roll world. Fortunately, he was unable to stay away from music for long and quickly dismissed his retirement announcement as the rash decision of a stress-and-substance-addled mind. He and The Attractions honoured a previous commitment to a European tour, even though they were minus a keyboardist: immediately following Elvis' outburst, an increasingly frustrated Steve went to California, where he was injured in a car crash, rendering him incapable of performing for a few months. 'My first solution involved the purchase of a Marshall stack and three hundred effects pedals and fuzz boxes', Elvis later mused. 'The debut of the 'Elvis Costello Experience' was a disaster which very few of the traumatised Channel Islanders who were subjected to it are willing to talk about. For the remaining dates in Europe, we were joined on guitar by The Rumour's Martin Belmont, who masterfully learned our adapted repertoire in double-time.'

After the tour ended, and with a recuperated Steve back in the fold, Elvis still needed to produce a new album. Sessions for the fifth album commenced in the summer of 1980. Adhering to that quaint colloquialism, 'familiarity breeds contempt', the band and their production crew decided to scout out a new recording locale. After discovering DJM Studios, the entourage, initially refreshed by the new atmosphere, discovered to their horror that the sound didn't suit their material at all: the studio was tailored to the tight and dry sounds favoured by rock bands of the early-1970s, but unsuitable for the sounds necessary for Elvis and The Attractions. This 'expensive error', as Elvis later called it, did little to help morale, and the sessions were, for the most part, fuelled by anger and resentment. With no tangible results apart from versions of 'Watch Your Step' and 'New Lace Sleeves' (both of which became part of the final product), the band cut their losses and went back to Eden Studios.

Elvis later recalled of the sessions in the liner notes for the 2003 CD reissue of *Trust*:

> Most days would begin with disenchantment at hearing the previous day's efforts, and a plan to repair to a pub at the end of the wonderfully-named Lamb's Conduit Passage would soon be proposed. Fortified by several pints of the cider that had fuelled our rehearsals, we then purchased a couple of flagons of the same, and the cycle of delusion and disappointment would continue until the small hours'.

Despite the general malaise that surrounded the band during this period, they achieved a relatively inspired performance on every song on *Trust*, as the new album was eventually called. Just as *Get Happy!!* was a zigzag from the slick pop/rock of *Armed Forces*, *Trust* dispels the claustrophobic whirlwind of *Get Happy!!* for a more structured attempt to create a more accessible record – not necessarily something that could be played on the radio, but a sound that was more of its time. The ever-rising popularity of new wave and new romanticism during the early-1980s meant that Elvis had to either move with the crowd or be outcast. While there was never a threat of him turning The Attractions into Duran Duran or Spandau Ballet, there was a perceptible change in sound on this album, toward the more angsty rock that he had perfected on *This Year's Model*. It wasn't quite *Armed Forces* – which was what the record company executives wanted – but it was more accessible than *Get Happy!!*.

There's a reason why all was not rosy in Elvis' writing: Margaret Thatcher had been Britain's Prime Minister for only two years and was already one of the most controversial premiers in Britain's history, and Elvis became particularly outspoken against the rule of the Iron Lady. *Trust* marks the first album for which Elvis would write and record politically charged songs, and the comparisons to early Bob Dylan folk records were inevitable. However, Elvis refused to allow his political beliefs to become the main focus of his career, and while he would always have something to say against political injustice in the United Kingdom and North America, he shrewdly stepped away from high-profile posturing and harping on about changing the world through music. 'The songs on this record', he later wrote, 'are loosely concerned with a kind of disenchantment that seemed to settle on me in my mid-20s. Certainly, the recent political swing to the right offered a gloomier sense of the future and provided the lyrics of 'Clubland', 'Pretty Words', and the unsubtle commentary on the new prime minister's enthusiasm for cold war posturing: 'Big Sister''.

There were still the preferred subject matters, however, with the other songs on the album written about disharmonious relationships, sexually-frustrated and impotent men, and 'the less attractive aspects of the triumph of supposedly civilised culture over instinct and passion – just yer usual pop song nonsense'.

Trust was preceded in December 1980 by 'Clubland', an impressive composition on its own merits but not exactly the most radio-friendly selection. Furthermore, the damage from the Columbus incident had been done, and the single failed to reach the UK top 40. The follow-up: 'From A Whisper To A Scream', didn't chart at all, while the US received 'Watch Your Step' instead. These failures did little to inspire sales of *Trust*, and despite being largely well-reviewed, the album didn't match the success of its predecessors, peaking at number 9 in the UK and 28 in the US.

> Elvis insists on experimenting with tone in an almost three-dimensional sense, developing his sandpaper rasp as much as the sweeter gears of his larynx – ***Record Mirror***

> (The album has) much of what made Costello famous, and little of what endeared him to me in the first place – ***Sounds***

> While the rest of pop was becoming increasingly simplistic, gaudy, and escapist, *Trust* was angry, complex, a confrontation – ***Melody Maker***

'Clubland' (Elvis Costello)

A-side, 20 December 1980; Peak position: 60

This double entendre-laden composition heralding *Trust* is a song that equates Britain's recent political shift to the right, with the seedy underbelly of an after-hours dive bar. The album's inner sleeve is brought to life here, with an unnamed patron telling the story of Clubland, which is home to doom, gloom, illicit sex acts, and corruption: 'The long arm of the law slides up the outskirts of town/Meanwhile in Clubland, they are ready to pull them down'. Elvis is at his punning best, quick to turn a phrase for the benefit of creating an even more sordid story.

When it came time to record 'Clubland', Nick Lowe was absent with influenza, so Elvis took production duties into his own hands. He later felt that the song 'probably never did recover from his absence. Although the arrangement was strong, I now see why Nick had some reservations about our master take upon his return to the studio. At the time, I was adamant that this was the version to be mixed, although I have heard the arrangement played to very much better effect on many occasions since'.

'Clubland' was released as the first single from *Trust* in December 1980, stalling at a disappointing number 60 in the UK: the first of Elvis' singles to not reach the top 40 since the first three singles from *My Aim Is True* failed to chart. Considering that 'I Can't Stand Up For Falling Down' had reached number four earlier in the year, this fall from grace must have been alarming for Elvis. Unfortunately, two further singles from the album – 'From A Whisper To A Scream' and the US-only 'Watch Your Step' – would also leave the charts untroubled. It must have been disheartening for Elvis that it took a cover of 'Good Year For The Roses' to bring him back to the top 10, if only temporarily.

'Lovers Walk' (Elvis Costello)

After the controlled chaos of 'Clubland', 'Lovers Walk' comes as a surprise, with a thudding drum performance and heavily distorted bass chugging away, as a deep-throated Elvis rattles off a list of love's infidelities, imploring the listener to 'look what love has done'. Elvis would later explain that several songs on *Trust* – including 'Lovers Walk' – dealt with 'the fact that I had come close to a terminal fracture in my marriage, (lowering) me into feelings of adult guilt and romantic disillusionment'. There's little melody here, with Elvis occasionally attacking his guitar as Steve Nieve pounds away on a fairly repetitive piano line, yet it's still an exciting and raw performance.

'You'll Never Be A Man' (Elvis Costello)

A song about aggression and sexual failure, 'You'll Never Be A Man' finds Pete Thomas' drums at the front of the mix, almost overpowering the other band members. However, each gets a chance to shine, in particular Steve Nieve, who pretties up the melody with his busy piano work. Elvis later categorised 'You'll Never Be A Man' – and most of *Trust*, for that matter – as a song of 'adult guilt and romantic disillusionment', though the man who sings this song is far more accusatory here than elsewhere, demanding that the woman 'give yourself away and find the fake in me', before backing off a bit and revealing that he doesn't 'wanna be the first, I just want to last'.

I would be remiss in not indulging the very few who know about my preference for the alternative take released on the long-deleted 2003 double-disc reissue of *Trust*, which sticks fairly close to the familiar version, though is slightly more tentative, sounding as if the band got the final performance on the next take. The reason I enjoy this rendition is simply because Elvis' voice comically and completely apropos of nothing, explodes in the second chorus on the word 'foreign'.

'Pretty Words' (Elvis Costello)

While most of the other songs on *Trust* dealt with deteriorating personal relationships, 'Pretty Words' (and later 'Fish 'N' Chip Paper') was a blatant attack on the media, with Elvis calling the song a 'gloomier sense of the future'. England's newly-appointed Prime Minister, Margaret Thatcher, was a drastic source of contention for the songwriter, though his words in the song are so deliberately obscured and muddled that it's nearly impossible to draw any coherent meaning from them.

Regardless of its confounding lyrical message, 'Pretty Words' is a sprightly performance, with many twists and turns that hadn't been heard on any of the *Trust* songs so far. As ever, a hardworking Steve Nieve delightfully colours the edges of the song, while a deliberately bored-sounding Elvis harps away on the subject matter. As on 'You'll Never Be A Man', Pete Thomas' drums are mixed as if to be the lead instrument, while a particularly melodic Bruce Thomas is regretfully buried among the clatter.

'Strict Time' (Elvis Costello)

This highlight finds Elvis at his punning best, with almost every line acting as a punchline to a joke that the listener has yet to be told. Another song of sexual to-ing and fro-ing between an aggressive couple, 'Strict Time' is set to a clattering, percussive rhythm, with Steve Nieve's piano and Bruce Thomas' bass duelling for attention, as Elvis delivers such lines as 'Cute assistants staying alive/More like a hand job than a hand jive' and 'You talk in hushed tones, I talk in lush tones/Trying to look Italian through the musical Valium'.

'Luxembourg' (Elvis Costello)

B-side of 'From A Whisper To A Scream', February 1981.

Perhaps the slightest and most forgettable track on *Trust*, 'Luxembourg' races along with little melody or deviation from the persistent rhythm. Meanwhile, a heavily-echoed Elvis – sounding much like his namesake – howls the virtually incomprehensible and meaningless lyrics, and such humorous wordplay as 'If this is a dog's life then you're the cat's clothes' and 'You're worried by her body, she's worrying about her bodily odour', is lost in the din.

'Watch Your Step' (Elvis Costello)

A song of careful caution, this song is deliberately paced slower than the preceding songs on *Trust*, sounding completely at odds with its predecessor, 'Luxembourg', but sounding similar to 'New Lace Sleeves'. Like that latter track, 'Watch Your Step' was recorded at DJM Studios in July 1980, which explains the dry and tight sound that is absent from most other songs on *Trust*; this aspect, which was evidently detrimental to other songs recorded at the studio, turns 'Watch Your Step' into a simmering boil, with a surprisingly-restrained Elvis wheezing out his vocals, occasionally sneering (especially in the last verse) as he issues his warning to the patrons of a bar. Reportedly written when the singer was barely 20 years old, the song is lyrically simple, with the most memorable verse directly addressing the pub patrons:

Broken noses hung up on the wall
Backslapping drinkers cheer the heavyweight brawl
So punch drunk they don't understand at all

The song was chosen as the follow-up to 'Clubland' in the US, instead of 'From A Whisper To A Scream', and was released in April 1981, making no impact whatsoever on the American charts.

'New Lace Sleeves' (Elvis Costello)

Elvis later called this 'among the finest of The Attractions' ensemble performances', though he was diplomatic in his description of the lyrics: 'That the song itself is mostly concerned with the tension between passion and the emotionally suppressing influence of 'being civilised', is an irony that we can all enjoy with twenty years or more of hindsight'. It's possible that he was referencing his extramarital affairs, by this time in his career, a recurring influence in his lyrics (reportedly, Elvis began writing the song at the age of 20, though he later claimed he completed it in time for the *Trust* recording sessions), though there's a more universal theme contained within the words for any couple engaged in a one-night stand and finding themselves going through the motions:

Bad lovers face to face in the morning
Shy apologies and polite regrets
Slow dances that left no warning of
Outraged glances and indiscreet yawning

'From A Whisper To A Scream' (Elvis Costello)

A-side, February 1981; Peak position: did not chart.
This energetic rocker was the first song to feature a guest vocalist on an Attractions recording. During recording sessions for the song, an increasingly hoarse Elvis was temporarily disabled from singing, so Glenn Tilbrook – vocalist, guitarist, and musical writer for Squeeze – was asked to deputise, his silky smooth voice disarmingly at odds with Elvis's usual gravelly growl. (Martin Belmont of The Rumour was also along for the ride, contributing additional guitar.) When Elvis' vocal cords recovered, he elected not to wipe Tilbrook's original vocal, instead trading verses in the style of Sam & Dave. Chosen as the second UK single from *Trust*, the song failed to chart, becoming the first Elvis single since 1977 to not enter the UK charts.

'Different Finger' (Elvis Costello)

Another song reportedly written before *My Aim Is True*, 'Different Finger' is the first outright C&W song to be released on an Elvis Costello album. ('Radio

Sweetheart' and 'Stranger In The House' walked so that 'Different Finger' could run.) Regardless of age, the song is a perfect counterpart to its frenetic bookends, 'From A Whisper To A Scream' and 'White Knuckles'. It even features a rare guitar solo from Elvis, occasionally duelling with Steve's tinkling ivories.

'White Knuckles' (Elvis Costello)

First it's different fingers; now it's time for white knuckles. One of the most instrumentally thrilling yet lyrically alarming songs on *Trust* – perhaps in all of Elvis' discography – 'White Knuckles' dances that fine line between clever wordplay and ill-advised shock value. Making light of domestic violence ('It doesn't matter if your face doesn't fit/There's no charge for changing it'), the song features Elvis as a horrified observer, witnessing the enraged man knock his wife around for seemingly mundane public displays of affection, whispering, and laughing. The woman is warned by her mother and sister, though she admits submission and (presumably) sticks around with the man. Chilling stuff, yet the musical background is the most enticing aspect: the song is set to a manic backing, with Pete's drums thudding like punches delivered, while Bruce's distorted bass kicks the song into overdrive throughout.

'Shot With His Own Gun' (Elvis Costello)

Elvis' extramarital affairs, substance consumption, and his meteoric ascension to success – followed by the swift fallout of the Columbus incident – had caused the breakdown of his marriage, though he would return home with contrition in time for a brief reconciliation. 'Shot With His Own Gun' came as close as Elvis could to publicly apologising to Mary for his indiscretions, though he distances himself (for the sake of the listeners' emotional attachment) by singing in the third person. Despite the personal and serious nature of the words, Elvis still throws in a half-joke after the second chorus: 'On your marks, man, ready, set', with 'man' sung barely without pause, though far quieter than his restrained and strained voice sings the remainder of the line.

The song was the direct result of Elvis having purchased a baby grand piano in early 1980, though, 'I was barely able to play it if anyone was looking', he later wrote. 'Steve Nieve's classical training was quite evident, as he provided a much more flowing and dramatic accompaniment than I could have imagined or mastered.' Indeed, Steve flies off into his own lyrical tangent toward the last quarter of the song, with the result being starkly beautiful.

'Fish 'N' Chip Paper' (Elvis Costello)

Another song that deals with the absurdity of the media (in particular, such rags as tabloid papers that thrive on celebrity errors and misgivings), 'Fish 'N' Chip Paper' is the most lightweight song on *Trust*, deliberately placed as a jolly chuckle after the more serious 'Shot With His Own Gun'. The lyric is reserved to two verses and a chorus repeated twice, with most of the song being made up of instrumental solos: Bruce's bass is the lead instrument during the verses,

Above: Elvis and The Attractions gearing up to take on the world.

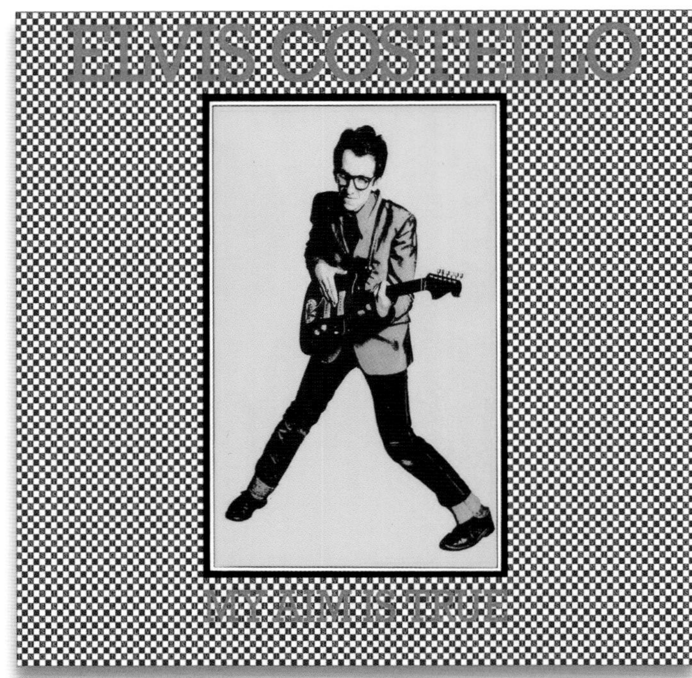

Left: Knock-kneed and geeky: Elvis's first studio release, *My Aim Is True*. (*Stiff* / *Columbia*)

Below: Taking himself not at all seriously from the *My Aim Is True* album cover shoot, 1977.

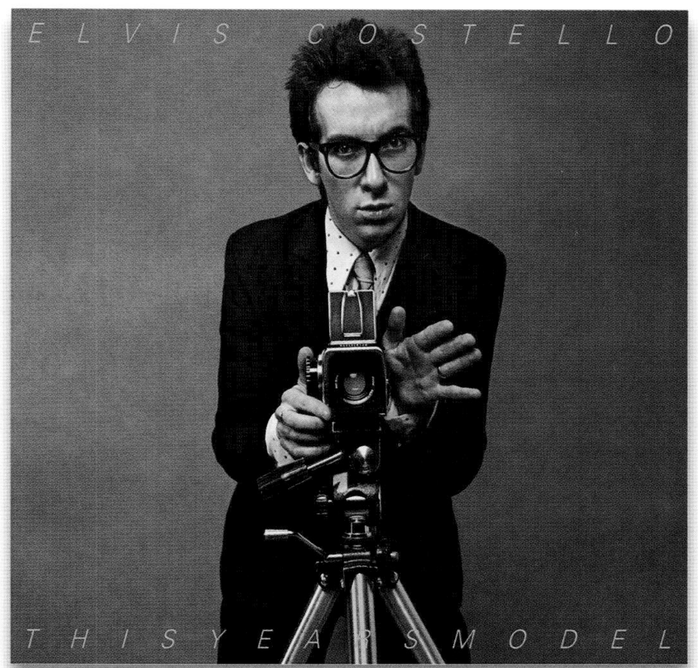

Right: Elvis discards the Jazzmaster and instead brandishes a Hasselblad for *This Year's Model*, 1978. (*Radar / Columbia*)

Left: The stunning European sleeve for *Armed Forces*, 1979, painted by Tom Pogson. (*Radar / Columbia*)

Left: Elvis and his trusty Jazzmaster on the stark set for the 'Pump It Up' promo video, 1978.

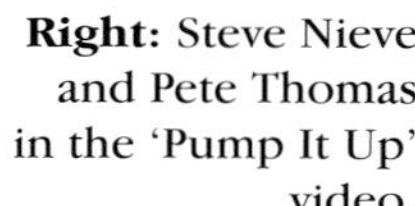

Right: Steve Nieve and Pete Thomas in the 'Pump It Up' video.

Left: The full band. Note Bruce Thomas's right hand, bandaged after incorrectly displaying how to break a beer bottle like a Hollywood actor.

Right: Elvis and the Attractions, pumped full of vodka and adrenaline, filming 'Pump It Up'.

Left: Same day, different song: the '(I Don't Want to Go to) Chelsea' promo video.

Right: ... and the single sleeve for that song, the first to introduce The Attractions. (*Radar / Columbia*)

Left: The Dutch sleeve for 'Oliver's Army', 1979. (*Radar / Columbia*)

Right: Tired of filming in white rooms, Elvis and The Attractions filmed the 'Oliver's Army' video in Hawaii.

Left: The Attractions in Hawaii with Steve Nieve strumming a ukulele.

Right: Few, if any, of Elvis's peers filmed their promo videos in such tropical locales.

Left: Putting the world to rights: Elvis singing 'Oliver's Army' on Top of the Pops.

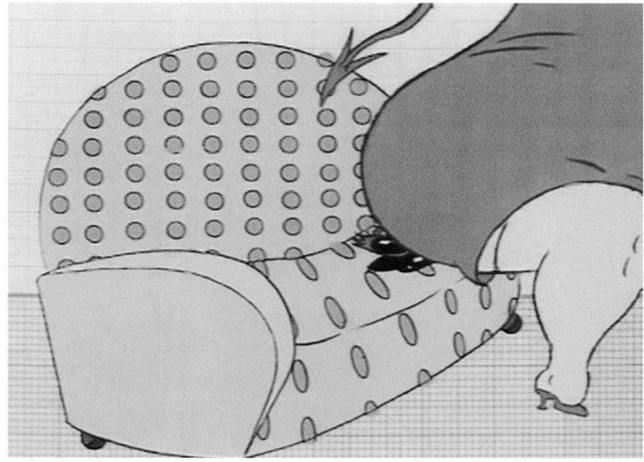

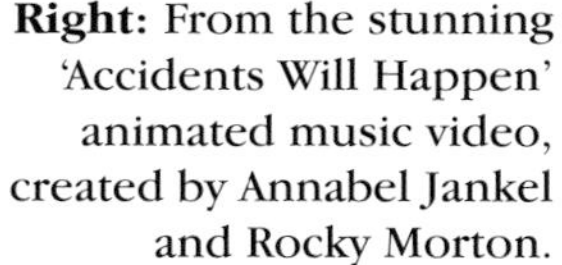

Right: From the stunning 'Accidents Will Happen' animated music video, created by Annabel Jankel and Rocky Morton.

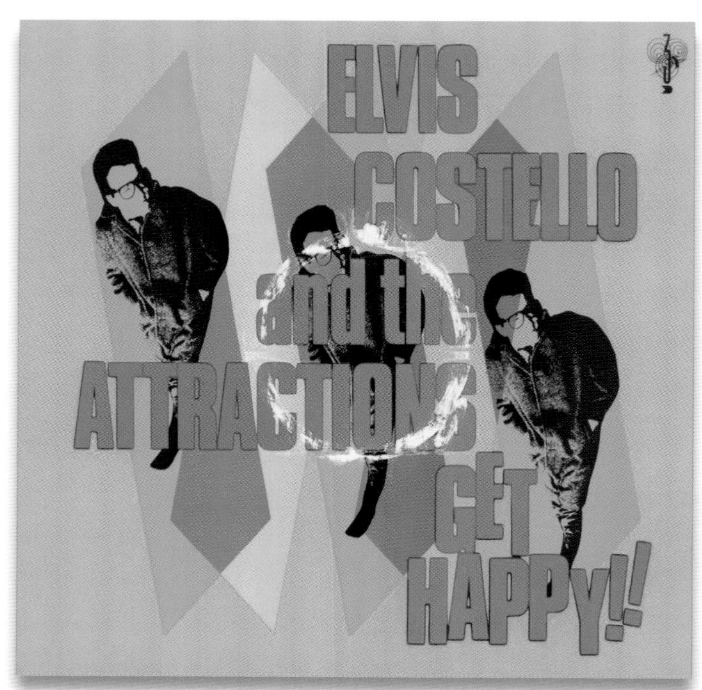

Left: Black and white world: Elvis and the Attractions go retro on *Get Happy!!* (*F-Beat / Columbia*)

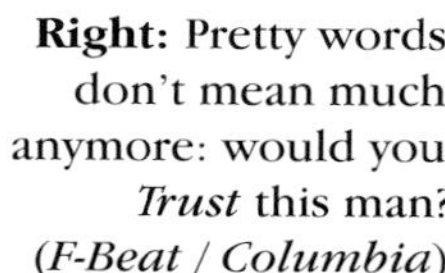

Right: Pretty words don't mean much anymore: would you *Trust* this man? (*F-Beat / Columbia*)

Right: *Almost Blue* came with a warning that it 'contains country & western music and may cause offence to narrow-minded listeners.' (*F-Beat / Columbia*)

Left: *Imperial Bedroom*. 'I thought I'd made this incredibly sunny-sounding record, a bright, more optimistic record.' (*F-Beat / Columbia*)

Left: Elvis (and Pete) head for the charts with 'Everyday I Write the Book', 1983.

Right: Steve Nieve, in a Kentucky Fried Chicken-inspired shirt, and 'Everyday I Write the Book' backing vocalists Afrodiziak.

Left: Claudia Fontaine and Caron Wheeler of Afrodiziak. Caron went on to greater fame as vocalist with Soul II Soul.

Right: Elvis on *Top of the Pops*, singing 'Everyday I Write the Book'.

Left: Pete Thomas, lost in focus on *Top Of The Pops*.

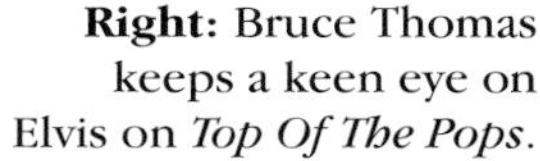

Right: Bruce Thomas keeps a keen eye on Elvis on *Top Of The Pops*.

Left: *Punch The Clock* gave Elvis and The Attractions their biggest success in years. (*F-Beat / Columbia*)

Right: ... while *Goodbye Cruel World* was designed to be their farewell album. (*F-Beat / Columbia*)

Right: 'He thought he was the *King Of America*': a dour ruler, 1986. (*F-Beat / Columbia*)

Left: Next time around: Elvis's tense send-off to The Attractions, *Blood & Chocolate*. (*Demon / Columbia*)

Left: Elvis with child backing vocalists for 'Good Year For The Roses' promo video, 1981.

Right: 'I found myself approached by what I then regarded as 'older women' who thought the record was 'very romantic''.

Left: 'I Wanna Be Loved', not one of Elvis's better covers, was redeemed by a superb music video.

Right: Executive producer Elvis joins Agnes Bernelle and 3 Mustaphas 3 on *Wogan*, 1985.

Left: Elvis treats Wembley Stadium to an 'old Northern English folk song' ('All You Need Is Love') at Live Aid, 1985.

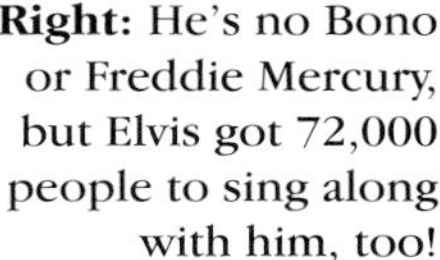

Right: He's no Bono or Freddie Mercury, but Elvis got 72,000 people to sing along with him, too!

Left: *Taking Liberties*, a US-only compilation of outtakes and B-sides. (*Columbia*)

Right: The UK equivalent, *Ten Bloody Marys & Ten How's Your Fathers*. (*F-Beat*)

Left: *The Man*. The first all-encompassing compilation of Elvis and The Attractions' singles, 1985. (*Demon*)

while Elvis delivers a lengthy guitar solo, trading off with Steve's sprightly piano and melodica.

'Big Sister's Clothes' (Elvis Costello)

The election of Margaret Thatcher as Prime Minister in 1979 outraged Elvis so deeply that, in a moment of befuddlement and anger, he penned 'Big Sister', the title an obvious nod to George Orwell's *1984*. Elvis' new composition was lyrically similar to Orwell's bleak portent of the future, though musically, it was too lugubrious and laboured to be seriously considered for inclusion on *Trust*. During the album's recording sessions in October and November 1980, a shorter version was recorded, though this arrangement was deemed unsuitable as well. With a slight lyrical tweak and the addition of a different chorus, the song was renamed 'Big Sister's Clothes' and recorded when everyone except Elvis and engineer Roger Bechirian had vacated the studio (hence the 'Nick Lowe not to blame for this one' credit on the record label). Elvis played every instrument – not only a conventional lineup of acoustic, electric, and bass guitars (with a bass line 'modelled on something by The Clash (which) might have risked an allergic reaction in certain members of the band'), but also melodica, tambourine, vibraphone, timpani, and an oddly-recorded accordion – and downplayed the anger in the original lyric, instead singing in a more restrained manner in order to emphasise the tragedy of the words.

Related Tracks

'Clean Money' (Elvis Costello)

B-side of 'Clubland', 20 December 1980.

Though it would later be rewritten as 'Love For Tender', suitably opening *Get Happy!!* in a manic fashion, 'Clean Money' was originally destined to be the opening track of *Armed Forces*, though its ramshackle arrangement would have been at complete odds with that album's slicker recordings. The arrangement owes 'quite a bit to The Beatles' 'White Album' rockers or, more likely, to the Beatles-influenced sound of Cheap Trick', Elvis later wrote in the liner notes for the 2002 CD reissue of *Armed Forces*.

> We threw everything at the song: a rock 'n' roll beat that is almost completely absent from the final running order, tracked guitar feedback, a guest background vocal from Dave Edmunds, plus a rare appearance from The Attractions as a vocal harmony group. It's hard to imagine the record opening with this belligerent tone rather than the blindingly obvious first line of 'Accidents Will Happen'.

The song was issued as the B-side of 'Clubland' in December 1980, and Elvis' original intention for it to open an album came to fruition when it was positioned as the kickoff song for the rarities compilations, *Ten Bloody Marys & Ten How's Your Fathers* and *Taking Liberties*.

'Hoover Factory' (Elvis Costello)
B-side of 'Clubland', 20 December 1980.
One of the most curious recordings in Elvis' early catalogue, 'Hoover Factory' was written in 1976 by a young Declan MacManus, as he passed by the eponymous building on the bus route to and from work each day. Lasting barely two minutes, the song features the peculiar arrangement of Elvis on electric and acoustic guitars, fretless bass, harmonica, and synthesizer, with several overdubbed Elvises providing spooky, wordless backing vocals. Recorded at Nick Lowe's Am-Pro Studios in March 1980, this version was issued as the B-side of 'Clubland' in December 1980, and on the *Taking Liberties* and *Ten Bloody Marys & Ten How's Your Fathers* compilations, also from 1980.

Almost Blue (1981)

Personnel:
Elvis Costello: vocals, guitar
Steve Nieve: piano, organ
Pete Thomas: drums
Bruce Thomas: bass guitar
Additional personnel:
John McFee: lead guitar, pedal steel guitar
Tommy Millar: fiddle
Nashville Edition: backing vocals
Recorded at CBS Studio A, Nashville, 18-29 May 1981
Produced by Billy Sherrill
UK release date: 23 October 1981; US release date: October 1981
Highest chart places: UK: 7, US: 50
Running time: 32:42

The fallout from the Columbus incident was swift, and any goodwill Elvis and The Attractions had earned since was destroyed by the relative failure of *Trust* and its accompanying singles. Relations between the band were strained. The exhausting cycle of recording and touring had taken its toll on the band, and Elvis, drinking too much and realising the end of his marriage was nigh, declared that he was going to take a break from songwriting and let other people's songs do the talking for him.

For the common Elvis fan at the time, his journey from punk rocker to country crooner seemed alarming, almost out of left field – yet, given the evidence, it really wasn't. Elvis had made no secret of his appreciation of C&W music, with *The Best of George Jones* in regular rotation on the Live Stiffs tour bus (until it was suggested he remove it so as not to 'confuse' any visiting music critics), while the Jones-inspired 'Stranger In The House' was a regular in the live set but infamously kept off *My Aim Is True* (once again, so as not to 'confuse'). He would also cite The Byrds' *Sweetheart of the Rodeo* and the Flying Burrito Brothers' *The Gilded Palace of Sin* as seminal in development and listening. On top of that, his estranged wife was a C&W fan, having introduced Elvis to many of his now-favourites, including George Jones: *Almost Blue* then could be viewed as a gift to Mary.

With his *modus operandi* in place and the majority of the songs he intended to record road-tested by the early spring of 1981, he reached out to legendary producer Billy Sherrill, to overlook the recording sessions. Sherrill, to his credit, had already worked with Elvis three years prior at a session to record a duet of Elvis' 'Stranger In The House' with George Jones, though Jones ended up a no-show, rendering the session useless. This time around, Sherrill wasn't too pleased to have been chosen to produce a snotty punk's midlife crisis. His aversion was to much of the material Elvis had chosen, and while he was committed to the paycheck, it became clear that he didn't think much of the four English poseurs.

Bruce Thomas didn't think much of the material, or of C&W in general, and played his parts through gritted teeth. The bassist was almost excluded from the sessions entirely, though not through any fault of his own. Just before rehearsals took place at Nick Lowe's Am-Pro Studios, Bruce was stricken with chicken pox. As a result, Elvis' original bassist of choice for The Attractions – Paul 'Bassman' Riley – was enlisted as a replacement and even took the flight over to Nashville in case Bruce's condition hadn't improved: though, happily, Bruce recovered just as sessions were about to start.

Riley wasn't the only guest to join Elvis and The Attractions: John McFee – first heard on *My Aim Is True* and an infrequent subsequent guest musician – was flown over as well, to provide lead and pedal steel guitar, while *The South Bank Show* filmed an in-depth feature on the sessions, showing a nonplussed Sherrill, a rather pickled Elvis, and his hapless band struggling to get through the sessions. (While it doesn't show anyone in the best of lights, it's still essential viewing for Elvis anoraks and can easily be found on YouTube.)

Elvis later described the album as being recorded when 'I was trying to rid the world of alcohol by drinking it'. While he was professional enough to not have recorded any of the material while drunk (keeping the mischief to after work hours), some of his song choices – both released and rejected – made it clear exactly where his state of mind was in the spring of 1981. On one occasion, requiring a much-needed boost of caffeine, Elvis took a gulp from a styrofoam coffee cup in the studio, only to discover that the producer had been discreetly nursing a cup of bourbon all afternoon.

At the end of a dozen days of work in Nashville, at CBS Studio A (not the more famous Studio B, which was closed down for renovation, much to Elvis's disappointment), Elvis decided enough material had been recorded and called an end to the sessions, leaving Sherrill and co-producer, Ron 'Snake' Reynolds, to finish up the album by overdubbing backing vocals from the Nashville Edition, syrupy strings, and fiddle from Tommy Millar, on many of the tracks. While many fans and critics were flummoxed that Elvis went with such a mainstream producer instead of a 'wilder individual … someone like Cowboy Jack Clement', Elvis maintained that he preferred the tension that Sherrill was able to achieve 'between the emotion of the singer and the smooth backing'.

It just didn't help that Sherrill's inspiration had seemingly evaded him, with his indifference resulting in an album that has polarised Elvis' fanbase ever since. While the lead single 'Good Year For The Roses' returned the band to the UK top 10 (the album itself peaked at 7, two positions better than *Trust*), critics weren't sure what to make of it. The *NME* was complimentary ('Costello and company cut through the layers of smart prejudice to find country music's enduring values'), while American critics like *Trouser Press* ('surprisingly clumsy'), *The Washington Post* ('Costello has invaded the trusting soul of country music and made a mean-spirited mess of it'), and *Creem* ('the heartbreak is drowning in a sea of clicked saphead, angst-vocal mechanisms'), had no love for the album. In the US, *Almost Blue* would stumble to its peak position of 50: Elvis and the Attractions' worst Stateside placement.

Elvis simply shrugged off the criticism, especially from America ('They didn't understand the motives behind it and they sort of resented us playing their music ... maybe it was the aftermath of (Columbus), maybe that was the final exorcism of all the unhappiness'), though he did attempt to get ahead of the blowback by placing a sarcastic, confrontational warning sticker on the Barney-Bubbles-designed sleeve (inspired by Kenny Burrell's 1963 Blue Note album, *Midnight Blue*): 'This album contains country & western music and may cause offence to narrow-minded listeners'. The only thing was, how could anyone be offended if they weren't buying the record?

'Why Don't You Love Me (Like You Used To Do)?' (Hank Williams)

Elvis explained in the liner notes for the 2004 expanded reissue of *Almost Blue* that at least one member of the Attractions (his diplomacy gives no indication who, though history has told us it was Bruce) found the restrained tempos of much of the C&W material, too much to tolerate; similarly, producer Billy Sherrill's antagonistic ambivalence towards Elvis and The Attractions was beginning to wear on the band. As a result, they tore through this Hank Williams classic, with a deliberately punk-ish arrangement meant to piss off Sherrill. Funnily enough, this snapped the producer out of his indifference, and he double-tracked the whole thing to give it more urgency. If only the rest of *Almost Blue* had sounded like this.

'Sweet Dreams' (Don Gibson)

A-side, 4 December 1981; Peak position: 42

Best-known as Patsy Cline's first posthumous single, released one month after her untimely death on 5 March 1963, 'Sweet Dreams' was a popular tune for interpretation, with covers released by Loretta Lynn and Emmylou Harris. But Elvis later revealed that 'our version really took off from a Jin Records B-side rendition, out of Louisiana, by Tommy McClain'. To date, McClain's is the most successful version, having hit 15 on the *Billboard* pop charts in 1966: even Elvis' rendition couldn't break the UK top 40 upon its release as the second single from *Almost Blue*.

'Success' (John Mullins)

Strictly honky-tonk, with John McFee duelling with Steve Nieve for attention, 'Success' sounds more like a pastiche of country music than being a truly affectionate nod. Even Elvis' pained vocal performance drifts toward parody at times. Happily, Pete turns in a spirited drum performance, pulling out the brushes for a sprightly shuffle, though one can imagine how bored Bruce must have been at the recording session. Discovered by Steve on an obscure Loretta Lynn compilation, 'Success' was perhaps performed with a tinge of irony, considering Elvis' marital difficulties at the time and the lyrical woes of 'success (making) a failure of our home'.

'I'm Your Toy' (Chris Ethridge, Gram Parsons)

Live A-side, 2 April 1982; Peak position: 51

First recorded by The Flying Burrito Brothers on their *Gilded Palace of Sin* album but released 'under the rather inelegant title of 'Hot Burrito No. 2', Elvis retitled the song to 'I'm Your Toy'. More profoundly, Elvis held an obvious affection, not only for this song but for its parent album, providing 'my first sustained interest in country music and (inspiring) a curiosity in the artists whose songs they covered'.

A live version – recorded 7 January 1982 at the Royal Albert Hall with the Royal Philharmonic Orchestra – is slightly superior to the album recording, with the saccharine strings balanced out by beefy brass. Released as a single in April 1982, 'I'm Your Toy' peaked at number 51 in the UK, with the single sleeve containing a note from Elvis: 'For those of you who enjoyed our fortnight's excursion into country music, here is a highlight from our Albert Hall bash with the Royal Philharmonic Orchestra, a new arrangement of 'I'm Your Toy' by Robert Kirby, plus some dusty sides from our Nashville archives. Yours blue on blue, Elvis Costello'.

'Tonight The Bottle Let Me Down' (Merle Haggard)

Elvis sings with unabashed glee while The Attractions finally wake up from their sleepwalking, delivering a spirited performance of a Merle Haggard paean to 'the one true friend I thought I'd found'. Steve Nieve once again plinks away on piano, though the real treat is hearing John McFee answering each of Elvis' lines on pedal steel. Another brief delight on an otherwise samey-sounding album.

'Brown To Blue' (George Jones, Virginia Franks, Johnny Mathis)

Another obscure country tune, originally performed by both George Jones and Johnny Mathis, 'Brown To Blue' is a baffling inclusion, as it sticks too closely to the original arrangement, and Elvis and The Attractions don't offer much to maintain interest.

'Good Year For The Roses' (Jerry Chesnut)

A-side, 3 October 1981; Peak position: 6.

Popularised by George Jones in 1971, 'Good Year For The Roses' opens side two in a languid fashion. The Attractions are unusually restrained, while Elvis' poignant tenor trembles with detachment rather than sentiment, delivering such lines as 'The lawn could stand another mowing/Funny how I don't even care' less with humour and more with muted numbness. Female backing vocals and John McFee's pedal steel guitar accentuate the recording, all heard faintly throughout the verses but climaxing to a full crescendo in the emotional choruses, with Elvis sounding like he's finally realising the full effect of his wife's departure.

'Good Year For The Roses' brought Elvis and The Attractions back into the UK top ten after a two-year absence. Released in September 1981, the single resonated with the public, peaking at number 6 in the UK. Elvis later mentioned his bemusement when 'I found myself approached by what I then regarded as 'older women' who thought the record was 'very romantic''.

'Sittin' And Thinkin'' (Charlie Rich)
Opening with 'I got loaded last night on a bottle of gin', Charlie Rich's 'Sittin' and Thinkin'' most accurately depicted Elvis' state of mind in the spring of 1981. The song had first been recorded by Rich for Sun Records (engineered by a young Billy Sherrill) as a jaunty C&W number, though Elvis and The Attractions made it their own and funked it up a bit, with the backing vocalists soulfully beefing up Elvis' lead.

'Colour Of The Blues' (Lawton Williams, George Jones)
More of a honky-tonk weeper than blues, George Jones' 'Colour Of The Blues' was an obvious choice for the album, considering its vivid lyrical imagery (unusual for a C&W song, but definitely up Elvis's alley) suited Elvis's emotional state of mind at the time.

'Too Far Gone' (Billy Sherrill)
A luxurious shuffle, with John McFee well to the fore, introduces Billy Sherrill's 'Too Far Gone', which the producer had convinced Elvis and The Attractions to record, though Elvis was familiar with Emmylou Harris' and Bobby 'Blue' Bland's versions. It's not bad overall, and Elvis ignoring Sherrill's advice to speak the second verse was a wise decision, despite the producer's attempts to convince him otherwise: 'There isn't a woman in the world who ain't a fool for a talking bit'.

'Honey Hush' (Big Joe Turner)
Written and first recorded by Big Joe Turner, 'Honey Hush' is the least satisfying performance on *Almost Blue*, with Elvis' voice straining uncomfortably while The Attractions sleepwalk through a lethargic arrangement. Luckily, there's a surfeit of contemporary non-album B-sides and outtakes on archival releases that fans can pick from to replace this: for my money, 'Your Angel Steps Out Of Heaven' or 'Psycho' are far superior choices.

'How Much I Lied' (Gram Parsons, Pam Rifkin)
Originally recorded by Gram Parsons on his first solo album *GP*, 'How Much I Lied' is a lovely closer for *Almost Blue*, with Steve Nieve's piano accompaniment taking off in his own direction. The band is unadorned by orchestration, backing vocals, and even John McFee, making it more listenable – and more honest – than most of the other songs on the album.

Related Tracks:
'Your Angel Steps Out Of Heaven' (Jack Ripley)
B-side of 'Good Year For The Roses', 3 October 1981.
This was an obvious choice for Elvis and The Attractions to tackle for *Almost*

Blue, considering both George Jones and The Flying Burrito Brothers had recorded their own versions. Wisely, Elvis opted against matching the original arrangement, instead restructuring it as a minimalist slow burn, with The Attractions getting their own moments to shine but staying out of each others' way. That Elvis relegated this stunning performance to non-album B-side status only confirms his fractured state of mind at the time.

'Psycho' (Leon Payne)

Live version B-side of 'Sweet Dreams', 4 December 1981.

Based not on Hitchcock's 1960 film of the same name, as has so often been rumoured, but on a then-recent (1968) spate of mass murders, 'Psycho' was written by Leon Payne and was first released (and immediately forgotten about) by Eddie Noack in 1968, before Jack Kittel brought it to number 114 in the *Cashbox* charts in 1974. Elvis and The Attractions' version – recorded at the Palomino Club on 16 February 1979 (with some contemporary vocal retouching) – was released as the B-side of 'Sweet Dreams', while a studio take from the *Almost Blue* sessions was released on the 2004 CD reissue of its parent album. A solo live version – recorded on 1 June 1981 at the Apollo Victoria Theatre in London – was released on the Royal Mencap Society charity album *Fundamental Frolics*, though this version has yet to appear on any archival reissue.

'Cry, Cry, Cry' (Johnny Cash)

B-side, 'I'm Your Toy' (live), 2 April 1982.

Written and first released by Johnny Cash in 1955, 'Cry, Cry, Cry' was deemed surplus to *Almost Blue* requirements, instead released as one of two B-sides on the live 'I'm Your Toy' 7' single.

'Wondering' (Joe Werner)

B-side, 'I'm Your Toy' (live), 2 April 1982.

First recorded by The Riverside Ramblers in 1936, 'Wondering' is the oldest song recorded by Elvis and The Attractions during sessions for *Almost Blue*. Deemed surplus to requirements, 'Wondering' was instead released as the second of two B-sides on the live 'I'm Your Toy' 7' single.

'My Shoes Keep Walking Back To You' (Lee Ross, Bob Wills)

B-side, 'I'm Your Toy' (live), 2 April 1982.

Recorded during sessions for *Almost Blue*, 'My Shoes Keep Walking Back To You' was covered by Johnny Cash, Loretta Lynn, and George Jones, among others. Elvis and The Attractions' rendition was issued as one of three B-sides on the live 'I'm Your Toy' 12' single.

'Blues Keep Calling' (Janis Martin)

B-side, 'I'm Your Toy' (live), 2 April 1982.

Written and recorded by Janis Martin in 1957, 'Blues Keep Calling' was recorded during sessions for *Almost Blue* but was instead released as the second of three B-sides on the live 'I'm Your Toy' 12' single.

'Honky Tonk Girl' (Loretta Lynn)

B-side, 'I'm Your Toy' (live), 2 April 1982.

Recorded for, but rejected from, *Almost Blue*, Loretta Lynn's 'I'm A Honky Tonk Girl' (its title shortened for Elvis and The Attractions' version, with the person narrative switched from first to third, as if anyone would mistake Elvis for a honky-tonk girl) snuck out as the third of three B-sides on the live 'I'm Your Toy' 12' single.

Imperial Bedroom (1982)

Personnel:
Elvis Costello: vocals, guitar; accordion on 'The Long Honeymoon'
Steve Nieve: piano, organ, harpsichord, keyboards, orchestration; accordion on 'The Long Honeymoon'; additional guitar on 'Tears Before Bedtime'
Pete Thomas: drums
Bruce Thomas: bass guitar; accordion on 'The Long Honeymoon'
Recorded at AIR Studios, London, November 1981.
Produced by Geoff Emerick, from an original idea by Elvis Costello.
UK release date: 2 July 1982; US release date: 2 July 1982
Highest chart places: UK: 6, US: 30
Running time: 51:04

In another attempt to prove that he wasn't willing to continue with a successful sound just to earn chart success (witness the drastic change from *Armed Forces* to *Get Happy!!*), Elvis decided some changes were needed when working on new material in the summer of 1981. 'We had made five albums between 1976 and 1980 (with Nick Lowe) … as well as touring together', he later explained. 'So we had all heard each others' jokes at least once by this point. In any case, I knew that I wanted to try a few things in the studio that I suspected would quickly exhaust Nick's patience.'

Elvis and The Attractions had been open to experimentation in the studio, though they didn't stray too far beyond what could be ably reproduced in the live setting. This time, there was a degree of ambition that needed to be explored, even if the result wouldn't translate well to the stage. Taking a relatively simple set of demos (recorded over two days in August 1981) and hammering them out in rehearsal over a week that October, Elvis and the band approached the arrangements with the intention of adding to them, as he explained in the 1982 promotional interview disc, *A Conversation With Elvis Costello*:

> But once we got into the studio, I started to have, in some cases, doubts, and in some cases, real radical shifts of opinion of what they should sound like. Even after we recorded some backing tracks, I started rewriting the songs, which is the first time I've ever rewritten material, which is possibly to do with the fact that I was actually in control, in the sense of the arrangements, beyond the instrumental arrangement, which obviously is a four-man job, with each of the guys working out their part. I obviously suggest the way I think it should sound to begin with, because it's my song, and then they work out their parts and then we kind of prune 'em back if maybe one instrument is dominating too much, or if it's not sounding the way it should. We actually put down some backing tracks and then I rewrote the songs over the backing track.

With this altered working method, the twelve weeks of recording sessions at George Martin's AIR Studios went a little better than hoped. Steve was given complete control to write arrangements that he felt would complement the music, with the most ambitious piece being '...And In Every Home'. As Elvis explained on *A Conversation With Elvis Costello*:

> 'What about if you wrote an arrangement for this, Steve?'. Because we'd always had this thing of talking about using horns and stuff, particularly on Trust... and then we didn't get around to it because it seemed like it was going to overbalance the track. But in this case, I said, 'Go mad. Write a really eccentric arrangement, you know, give full vent to your ideas'. Which is exactly what he did! Steve, on the other hand, did, in fact – there are some cheeky quotes in the arrangement. And he was just – we had the session, we did it in three sections, it wasn't all recorded at once. We did the strings first, and then the woodwind, and then the brass. And as the thing developed through the day of recording, Steve was looking over his master score and chuckling like a mad professor. And I thought, 'I think he's having us on here'. Because there are definite quotes, if you sit and listen to it, there is a quote from 'Eleanor Rigby' in there. There's also a quote from the '1812 Overture', there's a quote from 'Rhapsody In Blue' in there, and he was throwing them in deliberately. It is a humorous piece.

Indeed, on no other album was Steve given full reign to do with Elvis' songs what he pleased, and it's partly because of this that *Imperial Bedroom* is such a success. Elvis realised Steve's potential as an arranger, though it wouldn't be until over a decade later that he would come around to it.

While '...And In Every Home' is certainly the centre point of the album, Steve's fingerprints are elsewhere too. 'The Long Honeymoon' is quite an eccentric arrangement, with a trio of French horns subtly accentuating the humour in the lyrics, while the orchestration on 'Pidgin English' and 'Town Cryer' is astonishing, cinematic and splashed in technicolour.

In keeping with the ambitious arrangements, Elvis and Steve both explored new instruments, ranging from marimba, xylophone and celeste, to Spanish guitar, harpsichord, and accordion. Additionally, a fair amount of effort went into creating strange effects for Elvis' voice. On songs like 'Tears Before Bedtime', 'Kid About It', 'Little Savage' and 'Town Cryer', a startling vocal harmony effect is created to add weight to the words, though it's used more sparsely on 'Beyond Belief', 'Shabby Doll' and 'Pidgin English', where it sounds like Elvis is debating with himself – good Elvis vs. bad Elvis.

Apart from the usual tension that any Attractions recording session possessed, *Imperial Bedroom* was a relatively happy and productive period – at least, Elvis certainly thought so, explaining on *A Conversation With Elvis Costello*:

> I asked Barney Bubbles to paint a painting for the sleeve of *Imperial Bedroom*, and I thought I'd made this incredibly sunny-sounding record, a bright, more

optimistic record. And it had some humour to it, more overt humour. I didn't think it was a grim record, I thought the overall tone were things like 'You Little Fool' with the harpsichord and everything … And then Barney painted this dark, really dark, slightly malevolent-looking, very sexual painting, and I was like, 'Is that what it sounds like? It doesn't to me!'. I was delighted with the painting, and I actually really, really, really wanted to never have a picture on the sleeve again. My ambition was then to do a series of records and have him paint the sleeve, to paint the music, as it were.

Unsurprisingly, the album delighted critics, with the *NME* calling it, 'pop music organised to an incredible sophistication … Costello has finally achieved a synthesis of words and music that correlates to the duplicity of each. Every track leads its double life as a flawless pop song … This is miles ahead'. *Melody Maker* addressed the album's strengths while also acknowledging its obvious homage to giants before it: 'This record, accomplished as it is, has more cleverness than soul, more artifice than art … I expected more'.

Elvis later lamented to *Record Collector's* Peter Doggett in September 1995:

(The album) got some of the greatest reviews imaginable, which just goes to show how much they're worth, as it didn't sell more than any other record. The record company (F-Beat, distributed by WEA) couldn't find any obvious hit singles on it, though I think it had several – they just released the wrong tracks. The trouble all along has been that we make records and they sell them. And if you're making them, you're always looking for something new that excites you. But when I did what I thought was a really original record in Imperial Bedroom, the record company still thought of us in terms of Armed Forces. They hankered after that. So instead of releasing a bold piece of music like 'Beyond Belief' as a single – that would have marked this album out as a departure – or maybe 'Almost Blue', a ballad that was very heartfelt, they released 'You Little Fool', which is a good pop construction, but was the track most reminiscent of what we'd done before. It was idiotic. It was so cowardly on their part. Then, when the excitement for the album had been defused by that mistake, they released 'Man Out Of Time', which again could have been a bold first single. Then when it flopped they said, 'Well, we told you it wasn't a good record'.

The company still promoted it, regardless of their feelings toward the record, though this was met with considerable ire on Elvis' part: the campaign slogan was 'Masterpiece?', which Elvis felt lacked conviction. The relative commercial failure of the album (number 6 in the UK and 30 in the US: certainly better than *Almost Blue* and almost as good as *Trust*, but an obvious disappointment compared to *Armed Forces* and *Get Happy!!*) caused Elvis to rethink his strategy for approaching recording an album. That the singles from the album – 'You Little Fool' and 'Man Out of Time' –

both failed to hit the UK top 50, yet the cast-off cover of 'From Head To Toe' almost reached the top 40 was even more incentive for Elvis to reclaim the singles charts.

'Beyond Belief' (Elvis Costello)

B-side of 'Green Shirt', 4 May 1985.

Originally titled 'The Land Of Give And Take', 'Beyond Belief' is a menacing and foreboding introduction to *Imperial Bedroom*, summing up Elvis' current state of being with painful succinctness. He later wrote in the 2002 double-disc reissue liner notes that 'most 'private' matters should remain that way, but when the opening track is called 'Beyond Belief', and the key song of a record is entitled 'Man Out Of Time', you don't have to be a detective or a psychiatrist to work out what is going on'.

The original text of 'The Land Of Give And Take' was a lengthy rap with additional lyrics that were excised from the final version. Recognising the strength of the backing track (despite a pathetically hungover Pete Thomas, who nevertheless nailed his performance on the first take), Elvis altered some of the lyrics and slowed down his vocal performance (in the process, delivering the lyrics in a hushed, breathy tone as opposed to the more 'straight' original version) to almost half-time.

A clear favourite of Elvis', who – despite the song's non-appearance as a single release – has included it on most subsequent compilations, 'Beyond Belief' ended up as the B-side of the 1985 single release of 'Green Shirt', issued to promote the compilation album, *The Best of Elvis Costello And The Attractions*.

'Tears Before Bedtime' (Elvis Costello)

Heralded with a jaunty drum beat and percolating keyboards, 'Tears Before Bedtime' merges an upbeat melody with more sinister lyrics, the likes of which detail domestic discord. Though the lyrics are intensely bitter, Elvis cloaks this by occasionally slipping into sarcasm ('For the tears that you boo hoo hoo hoo, there can be no defence'), with the only instance that he allows himself to be regretful appearing in the final verse: 'Darling, your suspiciousness tortures me at night/But I can't excuse the cruel words that I use whenever we fight'. Seemingly written about his failing marriage, Elvis sounds almost gleeful at times, as if he were deliberately baiting his wife with his words.

This was the only original composition recorded during sessions for *Almost Blue* in July 1981, and the countrified version – complete with honky-tonk piano and pedal steel guitar – finally surfaced on the 2003 reissue of that album. Unsurprisingly, it wasn't a winner in that arrangement: the C&W backing works against Elvis' busy pen, and it was for the best that the song was abandoned. Elvis later credited Steve with 'his solitary guitar playing cameo in the final seconds of (the song)' – likely the guitar that mimics the vocal line as the song fades out.

'Shabby Doll' (Elvis Costello)

Another dark and murky recording, 'Shabby Doll' is introduced by way of a flanged acoustic guitar and Elvis' restrained yet brooding vocals. With the title taken from a music hall poster that hung in a hotel dining room (Elvis later remarked that he had been influenced by The Beatles' 'Being For The Benefit Of Mr Kite!', the lyrics of which John Lennon took directly from a fairground poster), the shabby doll in question is the narrator, who slips into self-deprecation pretty quickly ('And being what you might call a whore Always worked for me before/Now I'm a shabby doll'), though there's a certain humour to it, with Elvis even reverting to his punning ways with 'There's a girl in this dress/There's always a girl in distress'.

Special mention should be made of the closing minute, which features Bruce Thomas going nuts on his distorted bass while, behind him, Elvis whoops and hollers in a strained falsetto. It's astonishing to think that Elvis thought *Imperial Bedroom* was a bright and optimistic album when songs like 'Shabby Doll' prove the exact opposite.

'The Long Honeymoon' (Elvis Costello)

In March 1981, while on tour supporting *Trust*, Elvis recorded a piano demo of 'The Long Honeymoon' at September Sound Studios in Huddersfield, intending to send the tape to lyricist, Sammy Cahn, to try to come up with his own set of lyrics. Elvis later claimed to be going through a writer's block at this point in his career, which accounted for the *Almost Blue* album; before the year was up, though, he had defeated the block and was able to write material for *Imperial Bedroom*. Nevertheless, he still hoped for a collaboration with Cahn, which was in progress, before Cahn diplomatically removed himself from the project. Elvis later mused that Cahn 'was frankly bewildered by the music that I had sent to him on tape' and that he was 'seemingly surprised that I would be simply writing a song to record and not for a show or an event of some kind'.

With Cahn off the project, Elvis set about writing his own lyrics, which are amusing in a sad way, exposing a paranoid wife who suspects her husband has run off with her best friend. Another song like 'Tears Before Bedtime' – evidently written to bait his wife Mary – 'The Long Honeymoon' marries a depressing text to jaunty music with a slight Parisian tint, thanks to a wheezy accordion ('which took three of us to play', Elvis later explained: 'Steve at the keyboard – which we laid flat across the table – Bruce to work the bellows, and myself to wrestle with the beast and stop it from crawling onto the studio floor') dominating beneath Steve Nieve's hard-working piano melody, transforming Elvis' original demo from ham-fisted to slick and sublime.

'Man Out Of Time' (Elvis Costello)

A-side, 30 July 1982; Peak position: 58

'Man Out Of Time' sums up the fifty minutes of *Imperial Bedroom* in a little over five. Like 'Beyond Belief', it details Elvis' emotional spiral during the early part of the 1980s. He would later state that he was 'disgusted, disenchanted, and occasionally in love', and that the song 'was the product of a troubling dialogue with myself that continued through my more regretful moments'. He pinpointed the song's genesis to a hotel in Aberdeen, Scotland (where The Attractions played on 30 July 1981), a venue that had served as a retreat during an unnamed British political scandal. Drawing parallels to the guilty party who had fled to the hotel, with recent events in his own life, Elvis penned a sinister set of lyrics that mirrored the parting words of 'Riot Act': compare 'Would you still love a man out of time?' with 'But it doesn't look like I'm going to be around much anymore', and it's clear that Elvis was unsure what direction the future would take for him, his band, and his private wife and kid.

Musically, 'Man Out Of Time' is a scream – not in the figurative, humorous sense, but literally: it's bookended by an early recording of the song from November 1981, which was taken at a breakneck speed and features a hoarse Elvis screaming the words. 'I thought the song was too slow,' Elvis said in 1982, 'so we did a fast version of it, with the riff (heard) at the beginning and the end of the song, but then I thought that the song had too many chord changes to play at that speed and it sounded all rushed'. Recognising that this version was far too crazed and raw to work among the more polished performances on *Imperial Bedroom*, Elvis opted to bookend the slower version with the opening and closing of the frantic version.

Despite its extremely personal lyric matter and the fact that there wasn't anything else quite like it on the singles charts in the summer of 1982, 'Man Out Of Time' was nevertheless issued as the second single from the album in July 1982. It charted briefly, peaking at number 52 in the UK, six positions higher than 'You Little Fool'.

'Almost Blue' (Elvis Costello)

Taking only its title but none of the musical inspiration from the previous album, 'Almost Blue' is a standout track on *Imperial Bedroom* and one of the most accomplished pieces of music Elvis had written to date. The restraint The Attractions show is sublime. The marriage of Elvis' hushed vocal, Steve's superb piano arrangement, Pete's brushed drums, and Bruce's impressive ability to make his electric bass sound like a stand-up bass makes for one of the finest Attractions performances captured on tape.

Elvis later explained that the song 'was an attempt to write in a classic form, more so than any other song on the album … Also, the lyrical style is more akin to that particular era in that there aren't any words in there that you don't normally hear in lyrics written around 1940, except maybe in the bridge. The last thing I wanted to suggest was, in any way, nostalgia. That's why it doesn't have any more of an arrangement in terms of other instruments. I did toy with trumpet. Ideally, I would have liked to have played it myself; only I can't play the trumpet, so…'.

Elvis drew inspiration from jazz trumpeter Chet Baker's versions of 'The Thrill Is Gone' and 'Leaving', and was finally able to thank him when Baker

stopped by a session to contribute the trumpet solo for 'Shipbuilding'. As he later wrote in the 2002 CD liner notes:

> I gave him a copy of this album and suggested that he might listen to one track in particular. Although we met up again at his subsequent London engagements and even worked together on one occasion, he never mentioned the record again. It wasn't until several months after his death (in 1988) that I found out that he had been including 'Almost Blue' in his later sets and that it would feature in photographer Bruce Weber's documentary on Baker, Let's Get Lost. Chet's performance of the song before an indifferent film festival crowd makes for very uncomfortable viewing, but there is a wonderful version, featuring an extended trumpet solo, on a late 'live' album from Japan. He finally seemed to get what I hoped he would recognise in the composition.

'...And In Every Home' (Elvis Costello)

Perhaps Elvis and the Attractions' most ambitious recording ever, '...And In Every Home' featured Steve Nieve's orchestral score, which famed Beatles producer George Martin later oversaw. Conducted by Steve, the wild orchestral arrangement dominates, sounding like an uptempo equivalent to The Beatles' 'She's Leaving Home', though the lyrical subject matter couldn't be further from that forlorn lament. Elvis paints a picture of a disenchanted young woman in a failing relationship with a prison-bound boyfriend; she's in search of something more out of life but is in a constant state of arrested development ('She's only thirty-five/Going on seventeen'). Elvis later quipped that his one regret for the song's sessions was 'that none of us thought to capture the remarkable sight of maestro Nieve at the conductor's podium before the 40-piece ensemble'.

'The Loved Ones' (Elvis Costello)

Dominated largely by acoustic guitar and choir vocals sung entirely by Elvis, 'The Loved Ones' is a jaunty romp, though its bubbly instrumental performance betrays the dark lyrical matter.

Elvis told *Rolling Stone* in 1982 that:

> (That) is the hardest song to get over. Considering it's got such a light pop tune, it's like saying, 'Fuck posterity; it's better to live'. It's the opposite of *Rust Never Sleeps*. It's about, 'Fuck being a junkie and dying in some phoney romantic way like Brendan Behan or Dylan Thomas'. Somebody in your family's got to bury you, you know? That's a complicated idea to put in a pop song. I didn't want to write a story around it; I wanted to just throw all of those ideas into a song. Around a good pop hook.

'Human Hands' (Elvis Costello)

Elvis labelled 'Human Hands' as 'just a straightforward love song, as far as I can see' and 'a song of reconciliation', though the original lyric 'seemed too

raw and easily read, closing it off to the experience of others'. Set to a mid-tempo rhythm, with complex vocal harmonies reminiscent of many of Queen's greatest hits, the real star of the show here is Bruce Thomas, whose busy bass work helps make the song all the more interesting.

Elvis explained the song more on *A Conversation With Elvis Costello*:

> I don't think there's any big mystery to it, it's just I'd never written (a love song) before, and it sounds like it as well. It sounds like, never really getting to the point; it's not until the end of the song that I actually get to the point. It's about not being able to actually say that I love you, or maybe not saying it ever clear enough, or doing enough things that make it seem like you don't, you know? That's all it's about; it's a very simple song.

'Kid About It' (Elvis Costello)

Written on the morning of John Lennon's murder, 'Kid About It' wasn't intended to be a direct chronicle of the event, though Elvis later admitted that the line, 'Singing 'The Leaving Of Liverpool' and turning into Americans', was thrown in as a passing reference. Elvis also said that once the song started to develop, 'the meaning started to come out a lot more. I mean, obviously, from the title, it's sort of about lying; about abdicating responsibility as well. The girl in the first verse is lying to the bloke and then always running away from it. It's about running away, really, the whole song is about running away. Hence the bridge bit, it's about running away to sea, or the modern equivalent thereof. It's just a sad song about running away from everything'.

The song was recorded fairly quickly with The Attractions before Elvis took the basic track and adorned it with overdubs (guitar, vibes, and organ). He later explained on the 1982 promotional interview disc *A Conversation With Elvis Costello* that:

> I just had the mood thing in my mind, what it should sound like, and stayed there late one night and did it all ... so that when it came in, it had a defined mood. And it even had a chord in there that everybody said was completely wrong! But I held out for that as well because it then sounded like I heard it in my head. Although I thought it was a good backing track as a basic thing, I envisaged it sounding like this. And then the vocal arrangement on it was another thing again, until it started to develop and the song actually took shape while recording it, instead of the other way around.

'Little Savage' (Elvis Costello)

Set to a chugging instrumental backing with the relentless Thomas rhythm section mixed more prominently, 'Little Savage' 'is sort of a love song in a way, but it's a love song in spite of itself. So it's full of sort of, 'Oh, am I doing this right?', you know?', Elvis explained in 1982 on *A Conversation With Elvis Costello*. 'Most love songs are written either from a very firm conviction about love found or love lost, but I don't think there are nearly enough songs about people in the middle. And there are a lot of those people, so I think it's worthwhile writing 'em a few songs. People that turn from Mr Average into a Little Savage, you know, that's the whole point of writing the song, because those people have never had any songs written for them.'

The song had a difficult and laborious conception: originally envisioned as a slow song, it gradually progressed to a 1950s-style doo-wop song, which didn't find favour with either band or songwriter. Determined to make the song work, Elvis rewrote it many times over before hitting upon the final version. He deliberately wrote the melody to be sung in a lower register so that the higher response vocal would make more of an impact; the idea of adding layers of voices was initially entertained but quickly rejected. Elvis said, 'I did want the idea that it was like two trains of thought going on at once, so there's one voice singing and then these little asides come in'.

'Boy With A Problem' (Elvis Costello, Chris Difford)

At the tail end of the *Trust* sessions in early 1981, Elvis came up with the title, 'Boy With A Problem'. While he had written the melody on piano (around the same time as 'Shot With His Own Gun' and 'The Long Honeymoon'), he found that he was struggling considerably with the words. Considering the obvious connection with Squeeze (Elvis had just produced their *East Side Story* album, and Glenn Tilbrook had duetted with Elvis on 'From A Whisper To A Scream'), the singer asked their lyricist, Chris Difford, to help him out. This was not an isolated incident; Elvis found himself going through something of a writer's block at the time and was 'toying with the notion of abandoning some of the responsibility for the words'. 'Boy With A Problem' would be the only song on *Imperial Bedroom* to feature an outside collaborator; evidently, Elvis found his muse elsewhere and rebounded from his block.

The song is of a 'melancholic domestic mood' and tells the story of an obviously miserable married man, sinking into alcoholism and taking his anger out on his wife, realising his faults and expressing astonishment that she is quick to forgive him. When recorded as a demo at Eden Studios, Elvis sang all of Difford's original lyric, though by the time it was recorded properly at AIR Studios, he had tweaked some of the words. The exquisite backing – recorded when Elvis was absent from the studio and mailed to his home later that evening – complements the sombre mood perfectly, with Steve coming to the fore on piano, striking the glorious balance between retaining the feel of Elvis's original demo and adding enough flourishes to make it unique.

'Pidgin English' (Elvis Costello)

Deliberately written about the breakdown of communication between lovers ('Among the colloquialisms and lyrical puzzles ... there is a longing for the simple words to express love', Elvis later wrote, hence the whispered 'P.S. I love you' conclusion), 'Pidgin English' features some of Elvis' most confounding lines. Taken from the point of view of a frustrated man wishing to express his feelings, the song starts off in an almost straightforward lyrical fashion, though quickly degenerates into incomprehensibility.

> You go 'cheep cheep cheep' between bulls eyes and bluster
> Stiff as your poker face, keener than mustard
> From your own backyard to the land of exotica
> From truth society to neurotic erotica

Despite a word for 'love' in nearly every language, the narrator concludes by asking the object of his attraction, 'Have you forgotten how to say it in your Pidgin English?'.

Sounding like the more psychedelic moments from *Sgt. Pepper's Lonely Heart's Club Band* – bathed in swirling keyboards, raga-like guitar drones, and dripping with echo – the song also features a stately brass and woodwind arrangement by Steve Nieve, punctuating the chorus at integral moments, while the introduction, designed to sound like a sitar, was actually a National steel dobro. Elvis later commented that the acoustic Spanish guitar interlude – closely mic'ed to get extra bounce on the strings – was written into the song instead of being added as an afterthought.

'You Little Fool' (Elvis Costello)

A-side, 19 June 1982; Peak position: 52.

Written as 'a cautionary word to a young girl who is about to throw herself away on an unworthy fellow', 'You Little Fool' embodies all the production qualities of the album while transporting the song back to a time when psychedelic pop ruled the world. Opening with a beautiful harpsichord – that is the main instrument instead of just being used as brief cameo – the song sounds like a combination of something between classical baroque composition, The Byrds and The Beatles (the latter especially in the outro, using backwards tape effects as a nod to their 'Tomorrow Never Knows'). Elvis is in particularly fine voice here, duetting with himself at times, singing of the confused girl 'looking for an imitation of love', while her disapproving and uncaring parents, 'gives her some pills to choose/And says, 'Go and use your imagination'.

Released as a single a month ahead of *Imperial Bedroom*, 'You Little Fool' – backed with the non-album outtake, 'The Stamping Ground' – struggled to number 58 in the UK charts. Elvis later lamented F-Beat's relative safe choice of lead single, suggesting 'Beyond Belief' or 'Almost Blue' would have been more daring selections.

'Town Cryer' (Elvis Costello)

B-side of 'Man Out Of Time', 30 July 1982.

After 45 minutes of every range of emotions possible, *Imperial Bedroom* closes with this grandiose composition; 'a truthful if rather self-pitying lament', according to Elvis. 'Town Cryer' is taken at a deliberately slow pace, with Elvis' breathy vocal high in the mix. He was later quick to praise Steve Nieve's 'Philly-style string chart', which threatens to overshadow the Attractions' economic performance. The final minute combines string orchestration, French horn, and Steve's busy piano work, though Bruce's bass is just loud enough to remind us all that he's still there.

An uptempo version (alternately known as both the 'Version Discotheque' and the 'Barry White version') was recorded 'late one evening', according to Elvis' recollection, 'armed only with a wah-wah pedal and a beat group's attempt to imitate Barry White and The Love Unlimited Orchestra'. This is a surprisingly accurate description (more often than not, Elvis uses deprecatory humour to mask any shortcomings of a performance) and the recording is quite a hoot for anyone used to the elegant album recording: especially the brief overdubbed a cappella interlude, suggesting that Elvis had intentions for the song to be more than just a lark. This version was issued as the B-side of 'Man Out Of Time' in July 1982.

Related Tracks

'Big Sister' (Elvis Costello)

B-side of 'You Little Fool', 19 June 1982.

This early version of 'Big Sister's Clothes' recorded early in the *Trust* sessions, was rightly abandoned in its original beat group arrangement (instead, Elvis would record a disorienting solo version), though the multi-tracked chorus vocals throughout suggest it made it a lot further in the recording process than a quick studio run-through. All the same, it's hardly essential listening, especially considering the superiority of the familiar final version, but its release on the double B-side of 'You Little Fool' was a welcome one.

'The Stamping Ground' (Elvis Costello)

B-side of 'You Little Fool', 19 June 1982.

Recorded at an August 1981 solo demo session at Pathway Studios, 'The Stamping Ground' was part of a batch of songs submitted for *Imperial Bedroom.* But it ended up being surplus to requirements, and therefore, no Attractions version is known to exist. It certainly had potential, but the original recording is all that exists (the song was never played live). As such, its appearance on the double B-side of 'You Little Fool' (credited to The Emotional Toothpaste: a nonsensical *nom de plume*) was its rightful home.

'Imperial Bedroom' (Elvis Costello)

B-side of 'Man Out Of Time', 30 July 1982: and 'Party Party', 3 December 1982.

While 'Imperial Bedroom' is technically not a title track – having been written and recorded after the album sessions had concluded (though still a few months before its release) – Elvis later said that the 'lyrical possibilities of the title were too tempting'. Indeed, the stately title is translated well in this brief recording, which features Elvis on all instruments (including, as he later explained, 'comical percussion, the result of my first encounter with a Linn drum machine'), while he sings of a hateful and spiteful woman at her sister's wedding, running off with the best man moments before the ceremony, 'the casual acquaintance (leading) to an intimate bonsoir'. The song – credited to Napoleon Dynamite and the Royal Guard – was issued on the 'Man Out Of Time' 12' single in July 1982 and as the B-side of 'Party Party' in November 1982.

'From Head To Toe' (William 'Smokey' Robinson)

A-side, 10 September 1982; Peak position: 43

First recorded by Smokey Robinson and The Miracles, Elvis' version was recorded in February 1982 at Matrix Studios with the intent of releasing a non-album single. He based the arrangement on a little-known 1967 cover by the Merseybeat band, The Escorts, including The Attractions backing vocals (here credited as The Indulgences), resulting in a surprisingly fun and energetic performance. Unsurprisingly, Elvis later fumed when the single – backed with 'The World Of Broken Hearts' – performed far better than any of the singles selected from *Imperial Bedroom*: 'From Head To Toe' reached number 43 in the UK, while 'You Little Fool' and 'Man Out Of Time' peaked at 52 and 58 respectively.

'The World Of Broken Hearts' (Doc Pomus, Mort Shuman)

B-side of 'From Head To Toe', 10 September 1982.

'The World Of Broken Hearts' was originally performed by Amen Corner in 1967 and is one of the most obscure songs Elvis has recorded. Set to a minor key melody and with contrasting tempos, 'The World of Broken Hearts' is one of those instances where the B-side is as strong as, if not better than, the A-side.

'Party Party' (Elvis Costello)

A-side, 3 December 1982; Peak position: 48

Elvis has made no secret of being embarrassed by this song. Yet, despite that, 'Party Party' is enjoyable good fun, and paves the way for the bright, summery album that would become *Punch the Clock*. Written and recorded in late 1982 for the forgettable film of the same title, the song was credited to Elvis, the Attractions, and the Royal Guard Horns – Gary Barnacle on tenor and baritone saxophones, and Annie Whitehead on trombone – and features a rather lame set of lyrics (maybe I'm just out of touch, but any party that involves overdosing on aftershave and trying to slash your wrists, just doesn't sound like my idea of a good time) set to a perky and upbeat melody.

Surprisingly – and much to Elvis's chagrin – the song was issued as a single in November 1982, reaching number 48 in the UK charts (astonishingly, six places higher than 'You Little Fool', and ten higher than 'Man Out Of Time'), with 'Imperial Bedroom' as the B-side.

'Little Goody Two Shoes' (Elvis Costello)

Released on the Out Of Our Idiot compilation, 4 December 1987.

Eventually rewritten and rearranged as 'Inch By Inch' on *Goodbye Cruel World*, two versions of 'Little Goody Two Shoes' were recorded during sessions for *Imperial Bedroom* in November 1981. The first was a more uptempo reading that would later appear on the 1987 compilation *Out of Our Idiot*, and a second, a slower (and inferior) rendition that more resembled its eventual form. This version later turned up on the 2002 double-disc reissue of *Imperial Bedroom* and is, unfortunately, the one that is heard more. The earlier version was inexplicably left out of Rhino's CD reissue program, with its first release on *Out Of Our Idiot* remaining as its only release.

Punch the Clock (1983)

Personnel:
Elvis Costello: vocals, guitar, 'one-finger' Synclavier, Casiotone
Steve Nieve: piano, organ, Emulator, Fairlight CMI, Synclavier
Pete Thomas: drums
Bruce Thomas: bass guitar
Additional personnel:
Caron Wheeler and Claudia Fontaine: backing vocals
Jim Paterson: trombone
Jeff Blythe: alto and baritone saxophones, clarinet
Paul Speare: tenor saxophone, flute
Dave Plews: trumpet
Stuart Robson: trumpet and flugelhorn on 'The World And His Wife'
Chet Baker: trumpet solo on 'Shipbuilding'
Morris Pert: percussion
David Bedford: string arrangements
Recorded at AIR Studios, London, January-April 1983
Produced by Clive Langer and Alan Winstanley
UK release date: 5 August 1983; US release date: 5 August 1983
Highest chart places: UK: 3, US: 24
Running time: 45:08

True to form, Elvis and The Attractions had just released a magnificent album, but positive critical reception didn't translate to impressive sales. Understandably, this frustrated Elvis, who figured that a change in sound was due if it led to more units shifted. 'Well, that's what life's like', he grumbled at the time. 'We had a floating audience in America that only bought our records occasionally. We'd made two albums in succession that, to some degree, had lost ground. If you allow that contact with the mainstream audience to be severed for too long, you may lose the freedom to do what you want.'

A call was made to the then-in-demand producer and engineer team of Clive Langer and Alan Winstanley, who had worked with such acts as Madness, Dexy's Midnight Runners and The Teardrop Explodes. Elvis had worked briefly with Madness in late 1982, contributing vocals to their single, 'Tomorrow's (Just Another Day)', and must have felt a tinge of jealousy that the band had achieved so much commercial success – fourteen Top 20 UK singles between 1979 and 1982 – while he and The Attractions were struggling to get a showing in any chart. Langer was already familiar to Elvis and The Attractions. His band, Clive and the Boxes, had opened for them early in 1980 while he and Elvis collaborated on the stunning composition, 'Shipbuilding', first released by Robert Wyatt and 'covered' by Elvis on *Punch the Clock*.

'It was our chance to get reacquainted with the wonderful world of pop music and still maintain a sense of humour', Langer later diplomatically said. In December 1982, Elvis and The Attractions played three concerts to test out newly-written material, most of which would be recorded for the upcoming album. Part of Elvis' new direction involved augmenting the tracks with brass, which would prominently feature on the new album (The Imperial Horns: essentially the Dexy's Midnight Runners horn section rechristened as The TKO Horns). This allowed Elvis the opportunity to finally rearrange some of his older material, particularly songs from *Get Happy!!* and *Trust* that had been written with brass parts in mind, though time constraints had at the time necessitated other arrangements, usually by Steve. 'I had the idea of getting some horn guys in and they were available, so we (rehearsed) songs going back over the last two or three arrangements for those', Elvis explained. 'It worked out so well that I was keen to have them come in and play on the new album.'

The shows were a success and Elvis felt confident about the new material. In late January 1983, he and the Attractions along with Langer and Winstanley, started work on *Punch the Clock*. However, it quickly became apparent that the working methods of the new producers were drastically different from those that Elvis and the band were used to. Whereas Nick Lowe preferred to capture the moment instead of perfection, and Geoff Emerick had used the studio as a blank canvas (the less said about Billy Sherrill, the better), Langer and Winstanley 'favoured the 'building-block' method of recording: retaining very little from the original 'live' take (often only the drums) and tailoring each instrumental overdub to best serve the arrangement', Elvis later wrote. 'This system naturally precluded the spontaneity of our past 'happy accidents' but could yield startling results when the last piece was in place.'

Prior to the sessions beginning, and just before going out on the brief tour in December, Elvis held exploratory sessions with The Attractions and the Imperial Horns for an inconsequential song called 'Party Party'. Written for the plotless movie of the same name, the recording embodied a lot of what would turn up on *Punch the Clock*: bubbly production, loud drums, an infectious rhythm, and inconsequential lyrics with a memorable chorus. With this in mind, Elvis had a direction for the new album. It wouldn't win the same critical attention as his previous albums, but at this point in his career, it was time to start generating sales, and, as far as Langer was concerned, that was his job. 'I think he accepted that that's what we did as producers: hits', Langer later recalled. 'He always reacts against what he's done before, so we went for it. We tried to get singles.'

Langer realised he had his work cut out for him when Elvis presented him with a series of downbeat demos, recorded mostly on the piano, late in 1982. When Elvis and The Attractions premiered the songs live that December, they bore little resemblance to their polished studio counterparts: 'Everyday I Write The Book' was performed as a pastiche of The Merseybeats, while 'The World And His Wife' was a delicate acoustic number. Langer insisted that Elvis pick up a guitar and start writing more upbeat material. The process inspired Elvis to come up with largely disposable but catchy material like 'The Element Within Her', 'The Greatest Thing', and 'Let Them All Talk'.

Along with the newly-minted TKO Horns, Elvis and Langer opted to sweeten certain tracks with backing vocals by Afrodiziak (Caron Wheeler and Claudia Fontaine, the former of whom was later the lead singer of Soul II Soul, best known for their 1989 hit single, 'Back to Life'), adding a sultry smoothness to 'Let Them All Talk', 'Everyday I Write The Book', 'TKO (Boxing Day)' and 'Charm School'. In fact, the overall sound of *Punch the Clock* smooths out the rough edges of The Attractions' road-perfected and substance-fuelled grit. While they had been making natural progressions toward maturity – between *This Year's Model* and *Imperial Bedroom* – *Punch the Clock* stripped their identity down to its barest essentials before adding heavy layers of slickness. It's not that *Punch the Clock* is any worse than its predecessors; it's that the album is simply a drastic shift towards commerciality. Upon its release in August 1983, *Punch the Clock* raced up the UK charts to number 3: Elvis and The Attractions' best showing since *Get Happy!!*; while it returned them to the top 30 in the US, reaching 24, undoubtedly helped by an extensive live campaign across America.

Perversely, even with chart success and increased concert attendance, Elvis was still uncertain about the path he had taken. The public liked the album, and the critics were suspiciously pleased with it (if a bit cautious), but Elvis maintained that the album was of its time but otherwise had little merit. While *Punch the Clock* would have been a nice and perfectly acceptable one-off, Elvis made the mistake of inviting Langer and Winstanley back for the follow-up album – hardly a detraction of their obvious talents, but the circumstances had changed drastically a year on, with an internally combusting Attractions, and a newly-divorced Elvis restless to escape the confines of the band format but hesitant to pull the trigger.

'Let Them All Talk' (Elvis Costello)

A-side, 2 September 1983; Peak position: 59

Beginning the latest album with a blast of horns and thundering drums, 'Let Them All Talk' is a curiously upbeat song that assaults the listener with a riff as insistent as a jackhammer. Though lyrically slight – the song is about the joys of marriage while time slips away – the chorus is catchy, and the energy infectious enough to make it a suitable opener.

Not surprisingly, given its energy, 'Let Them All Talk' was chosen as the second single from *Punch the Clock* ('Pills And Soap' was added to the album as an afterthought, having been released as a single nearly three months prior). Considering the rather pedestrian lyrics – which less tell a story and seem to be designed more to fit the riff – it's obvious that Elvis was going for radio-play over substance: ironic, considering the lines, 'Listening to the sad songs that the radio plays/Have we come this fa-fa-fa to find a soul cliché?'. Of course, radio-play was the plan from the start with *Punch the Clock.* But while 'Everyday I Write The Book' reached the top 30 in the UK, 'Let Them All Talk' struggled, peaking at a disappointing 59 upon its release in September 1983.

'Every Day I Write The Book' (Elvis Costello)

A-side, 1 July 1983; Peak position: 28

'Written in a spare ten minutes on tour as a spoof of a Merseybeat tune', Elvis later explained of his best-known single – whether he liked it or not. 'In rehearsal, Clive guided us towards an arrangement that was unlike anything we had ever recorded. Although we borrowed a few touches from the R&B styles of the day, I have witnessed, first-hand, the record's ability to clear a nightclub dance floor in seconds.'

Elvis originally envisioned his newest song as a Merseybeats-inspired arrangement and debuted it as such during his Christmas 1982 shows in Liverpool and London. An attempt at this arrangement was made in the studio (as was an unreleased but bootlegged 'reggae' version, in the loosest sense of the genre possible), but Langer flexed his clout and suggested a more radio-friendly arrangement. This meant building the song, instrument by instrument, to achieve something that could be pulled apart, stripped down, and built back up at will. This came in handy for Elvis' first 'proper' extended remix ('Pills And Soap' had been extended by 26 seconds by simply repeating a section over again, amounting to little more than a cheeky joke), which inevitably fell victim to the studio trickery of other 12' extended versions of the day.

The song itself, regardless of version, is little more than an enjoyable slice of commercial pop/rock with a clever set of lyrics that equate a relationship to the tortured process of writing a book. Documenting the inevitable blossoming breakdown of a relationship, Elvis cleverly takes the stance of an author working on a book, turning the story into a novel, with particular incidences reduced to a simple blurb ('The way you walk/The way you talk, and try to kiss me, and laugh/In four or five paragraphs'), while remembering words said in moments of heated passion ('All your compliments and your cutting remarks/Are captured here in my quotation marks').

Released as the first proper single from *Punch the Clock* in July 1983, 'Everyday I Write The Book' gave Elvis and The Attractions their first top 30 single since 'Good Year For The Roses'. More importantly, Elvis finally achieved his goal of a hit single in North America, where it peaked at 36 on the *Billboard* Hot 100 chart and 33 in *Billboard*'s Mainstream Rock chart.

'The Greatest Thing' (Elvis Costello)

Despite the album's bright and shiny sheen, Elvis wrote many of the *Punch the Clock* songs on the piano in a melancholy, downbeat manner. When he presented the demos to his new production team, Clive Langer in particular, suggested he close the piano lid and instead pick up a guitar to write some more upbeat songs. 'The Greatest Thing' was one of the first songs to materialise, and while Elvis would remain 'allergic to the happy ending ... I managed a pair of proud and wishful songs on love and marriage', with 'Let Them All Talk', the second result.

'The Greatest Thing' doesn't say much more than how great being married and in love is; there's no discord, no misery, and no thoughts of anger or disharmony. Elvis even offers a bit of advice – 'Punch the clock and in time you'll get pulled apart/If you're married on paper and not in your heart' – and counters that not all marriages are perfect: 'So girls like that above described/ Are not so easily bribed/With a white frock and a ring'.

'The Element Within Her' (Elvis Costello)

Despite the *joie de vivre* of the first three songs, *Punch the Clock* descends into pop confectionary with 'The Element Within Her', another track that was the result of producer Clive Langer's challenge to achieve fewer melancholy songs. Elvis later admitted as much in the 2003 CD reissue liner notes: 'Being in a fairly feckless frame of mind, I had dashed off a couple bright pop tunes that didn't have much else to them. The chorus of 'The Element Within Her' consisted entirely of the immortal words, 'La-la-la, la-la-la, la-la-la'. Despite the Merseybeat arrangement and the Beatlesque vocal harmonies, 'The Element Within Her' remains the weakest song on *Punch the Clock*, an opinion seemingly shared by Elvis, who has played the song exactly twice in his career: once in December 1983 and again in May 2011.

'Love Went Mad' (Elvis Costello)

Much like 'The Element Within Her', 'Love Went Mad' is a bright, poppy tune that's heavy on production and short on substance. Unlike its predecessor, though, this song's arrangement works a little better, despite the almost grating keyboard performance from Steve Nieve. The drums threaten to overpower, Elvis sounds noncommittal, and the lyrics about a failed relationship are largely superfluous (though there is one great line: 'I wish you luck with a capital 'F'').

Elvis wasn't particularly enamoured with the song, later writing: 'Certainly, even a slight and lyrically-laboured song about life in a nuclear shelter such as 'Love Went Mad', is clearly musically rooted in the 1960s, and I suppose Clive (Langer) saw it as his job to bring us more into the moment, hence the voguish arrangement that the song barely deserved'.

Perhaps reflecting his apparent disdain for the song, Elvis has prevented 'Love Went Mad' from ever appearing in any setlist. It's one of a small handful of songs that he has never performed or even referenced in the live setting.

'Shipbuilding' (Elvis Costello, Clive Langer)

In March 1982, a political conflict between Argentina and the United Kingdom erupted, with the former's intention to forcibly reclaim the Falkland Islands from the British. Though this never led to a full-scale war – neither side officially declared the act of war on the other – it did spark its share of outrage around the world, especially due to the senseless loss of 258 British and 649 Argentine lives. Protest records were released by the likes of Joe Jackson, Gang of Four and New Model Army, while Roger Waters was affected enough to devote an entire album to the war: Pink Floyd's *The Final Cut*.

Elvis was equally affected, writing in the 2003 CD reissue liner notes:

> I thought I'd seen it all in the British media coverage: grown men drooling over the hardware, the sick illusion of invincibility before H.M.S. Sheffield was hit by an Exocet missile, The Sun's 'Gotcha' headline when 300 Argentine sailors drowned when the Belgrano went down, the construction of the odd heroic myth to cheer everyone up after a series of blunders had led to a pointless and brutal slaughter of Welsh Guards, and, of course, the real star of the show: the prime minister arriving on our screens each day as if directly from the theatrical costumiers. Sometimes as Boadicea. Sometimes as Britannia. Oh! I nearly forgot the raving lunatic who reared up from the Tory back-benches to suggest a nuclear attack on Buenos Aires ... Most of the above was beyond words, but the notion that this might really drag on and become a war of attrition, seemed as believable as anything else. Ships were being lost. More ships would soon be needed. So: 'Welcome back the discarded men of Cammell Laird, Harland and Wolff and Swan Hunter. Boys are being lost. We need more boys. Your sons will do... just as soon as those ships are ready'.

Despite the setup, 'Shipbuilding' is not a protest record against the Falklands Conflict per se, though it was directly inspired by the events. In late 1982, producer Clive Langer asked Elvis to write some lyrics to a piano melody he had written, with the intent of giving the song to Robert Wyatt. Langer was disappointed with the first set of lyrics he had drafted himself and, after running into Elvis at a party at Nick Lowe's house, asked him to see what he could come up with. The result was 'Shipbuilding', indeed one of Elvis' finest lyrics ever.

Written as 'less of a protest song than a warning sign', the story is told from the point of view of an unemployed shipbuilder, who is conflicted when told the yards will be opening again to produce more ships to send troops off to fight a pointless war. The news becomes personal when his son also alerts him that he'll be fighting in the conflict ('Dad, they're going to take me to task/But I'll be back by Christmas': an empty, hollow promise that recalls the claims of World War I in August 1914, when troops were told the war would be over in a few months), and seemingly ends in despair for the working man: 'It's just a rumour that was spread around town/A telegram or a picture postcard/Within weeks they'll be reopening the shipyard/And notifying the next of kin'.

Wyatt's version of 'Shipbuilding' was released in late 1982, produced by Langer, Alan Winstanley and Elvis; this version reached 35 in the UK charts, '(reaching) many people in Britain', as Elvis later explained. 'Despite being daunted by the prospect of 'covering' the song, I wanted to include it on *Punch the Clock* so that it would be heard by a wider audience. As Steve Nieve played the piano on Robert's version, I thought we should feature a trumpet soloist on our rendition.'

The words are touching and marry poignantly to Langer's effective melody: his co-credit often unfairly overlooked. The trumpet feature was Elvis' idea, and though Miles Davis was his ideal guest, that changed quickly, explaining in the 2003 CD reissue liner notes:

> I opened the paper to find that Chet Baker was playing a hurriedly announced residency at The Canteen. I went alone to find Chet in a wonderful musical form despite the presence of several drunken bores who would loudly call for more booze in the middle of some of his most delicate playing. You got the feeling that this happened most nights, but it seemed particularly appropriate that the main culprit was said to be one of London's leading jazz critics. Between sets, I introduced myself to Chet, who was wandering about in the club untroubled by patrons. There is no false modesty in saying he had no idea who I was. Why the hell should he? However, he accepted my invitation to come and play on the 'Shipbuilding' session the next day. I mentioned a fee. He said 'Scale'. I think I probably doubled it ... It was a tense but rewarding session. Chet took a little time to grasp the unusual structure of the song, but once he had it, he played beautifully, even if he looks pretty deathly in the studio photos. I'd also say it was one of The Attractions' very best performances.

Bruce Thomas agreed, considering it 'the pinnacle of our ensemble playing, with the catalyst as Chet Baker. It's the way he follows the bass line through the solo, he's really, really listening, and even though he was a wreck of a carcass of a human being, he was the finest musician that we ever worked with'. Indeed, while Elvis would later (characteristically) downplay his own version ('I don't believe (it), vocally, is worth a carrot next to him'), it's a gorgeous recording, undoubtedly the highlight of *Punch the Clock*, and a stunning contrast to the sunnier, more disposable pop tunes – a stark reminder that however escapist and carefree pop culture allows us to be, reality lurks just ahead.

'TKO (Boxing Day)' (Elvis Costello)

Coming after the glorious solemnity of 'Shipbuilding', the second side opener, 'TKO (Boxing Day)', is memorable enough with the horn section blasting away on an infectious riff. But the song becomes wearing after a while, especially the lengthy outro, with backing vocalists, Afrodiziak, moaning away to little effect. Elvis makes clever use of the 'total knockout' abbreviation in the lyrics (the Boxing Day he's talking about isn't the day after Christmas), but it comes as a shock to hear a song that so gleefully romanticises domestic violence, especially mixed among songs with happier endings. This was intentional, according to Elvis, drawing parallels between a pair of 'proud and wishful songs on love and marriage – 'The Greatest Thing' and 'Let Them All Talk' – and a couple about the ugly truth: 'Mouth Almighty' and 'Boxing Day''.

'Charm School' (Elvis Costello)
A return to Clubland ('Happy days are here again/And all the drinks half price'), with an underlying theme of despair in a failed relationship, 'Charm School' starts off promisingly enough with a groovy Bruce Thomas bass line and a tempo slower than the relatively upbeat previous material. But the song suffers from its production: the drums overpower, the keyboards irritate, and the silky smooth backing vocals are superfluous.

'The Invisible Man' (Elvis Costello)
Another upbeat song written to order by producer Clive Langer, 'The Invisible Man' was cobbled together with unused lyrics from a trio of unreleased songs ('Twenty-Five to Twelve', 'Seconds Of Pleasure' and 'I Turn Around'), and it's obvious: there's no distinct story or narrative, with a deluge of words thrown in because they seemingly worked well enough. What saves 'The Invisible Man' from its baffling story, is the brass-heavy arrangement, written deliberately by Elvis to be a feature for the TKO Horns, though Elvis' acoustic demo recording (released on the 2003 double-disc reissue of *Punch the Clock*) has a certain charm to it as well.

'Mouth Almighty' (Elvis Costello)
Punch the Clock starts to sound rather samey as the back half progresses, making for a rather exhausting listen. This is a shame for 'Mouth Almighty', because it tells a cautionary (perhaps autobiographical?) tale of saying the wrong thing too many times, with clever wordplay ('All the pavements for miles around are littered with your footprints'; 'So I threw away the rose and held on to the thorn'), though it is marred by Clive Langer's contemporary, kitchen-sink production. It doesn't help that Elvis sounds astonishingly bored here, only coming to life in the chorus; even then, Langer has smoothed out the rougher edges of a sneer with echo. The one surprise is Elvis's guitar work: listen for some scorching guitar lines in the choruses (frustratingly mixed too low), while he provides a rare solo in the extended outro.

'King Of Thieves' (Elvis Costello)
Lyrically speaking, 'King Of Thieves' is one of Elvis' more clever and underrated songs. Telling the story of 'the trials of a blacklisted scriptwriter', the song is a chilling reminder of the McCarthy era and an ominous portent of what the future could hold; remember, 1984 was only a year away, and elements of George Orwell's bleak novel seemed to be coming true at the time of the song's writing. The song is well-written, with some clever lines, but the arrangement drags it down to become nearly unlistenable: the Attractions hang onto a frankly boring and unmelodic riff, and while Steve does his best to liven up the proceedings, it's a wasted opportunity.

'Pills And Soap' (Elvis Costello)
A-side, 27 May 1983; Peak position: 16

Inspiration for Elvis' lyrics usually came from real-life situations that people put themselves (or himself) into, but it took a 1981 movie titled *The Animals Film* and Grandmaster Flash and Melle Mel's 'The Message' to inspire Elvis' first true protest record. Indeed, these two sources may make strange bedfellows, which explains the equally strange record created, but Elvis was clearly troubled. The film itself 'was a long, harrowing portrayal of man's abuse of animals as pets and exhibits in factory farming and scientific research. It didn't take much to extract that we are willing to do unto each other as we do to the animals. Beyond that, it was a catalogue of the lovely times with the tabloid press just beginning to hone their skills of assassination, exploitation, and phoney indignation, the country's blind, sad affair with the lucky family in the palace and the new rank breath of jingoism'.

'Pills And Soap' was written with a broader target in mind and in an attempt to sway the British public from voting the Conservatives back into office. It was no secret that Elvis abhorred Margaret Thatcher as a leader and as a person, but it's interesting to note that the song isn't necessarily anti-Tory, nor is it pro-Labour; it's merely a combination of disappointment and disgust with what people will subject themselves to, and, the larger the crowd, the more mindless they become. This ties in with the anti-media diatribe that surfaces in the first and third verses, which an annoyed Elvis admonishes for profiting from other peoples' suffering and misery. It's only gotten worse since.

The record's sound is sparse and eerie, which creates a chilling effect when coupled with the lyrics: to an echoed drum machine beat, Steve Nieve's piano clatters out a derivation of a melody Elvis had been working on, sounding 'something like Ramsey Lewis… or Mose Allison… or Dave Brubeck might play… ('The Message') was the first rap record that I had encountered that was any more than an invitation to dance. It spoke about ugly life … I could not adopt such a vocal delivery, but I wanted to set my litany to a drum machine beat. So I turned the piano part over to Steve Nieve (who could actually play it) and switched on the device'.

Proving that he could move quickly when motivated, Elvis recorded the song on Wednesday 18 May 1983, with acetates pressed the next day. By Friday 27 May, the single was in the shops, with Elvis even personally delivering copies to the music press that day. 'The ability to achieve all this so quickly had everything to do with the fact that I was not, for the moment, being distributed by a major record label', he later explained. ''Pills And Soap' – credited to The Imposter, a 'Fairley/Imposter Production' – appeared on IMP Records: a Demon Records imprint. It was released for a limited period only and melodramatically deleted on the eve of the 1983 general election.' Not quite: while it was claimed that only 15,000 copies were pressed, in actuality, 160,000 were released. The single – backed with an 'extended' version (simply just a few beats of the intro and the chorus of 'Give me the needle/Give me the rope' before 'Four and twenty crowbars' sung four times instead of twice) – reached number 16 in the UK charts and was Elvis' best chart placing since 'Good Year For The Roses'. 'The need to reissue it the following day on a celebratory red vinyl 12', sadly never arose', he later lamented.

'The World And His Wife' (Elvis Costello)

Elvis wisely decided not to end *Punch the Clock* – his most deliberately accessible and chart-friendly album – on such a bleak note as 'Pills and Soap'. According to him, 'The World And His Wife' was 'rewritten from a solemn folk song about a drunken family gathering, into a bilious knees-up with the (TKO) horns playing their part in the scene'. For anyone who had lost faith in (or gotten bored with) the second half of *Punch the Clock* but had decided to stick it out nonetheless, 'The World And His Wife' is a welcome reward: the Attractions sound like they're having a great time, while the TKO Horns inject a bold and fresh feeling into the song. Even Elvis sounds like he's having a blast, gleefully spitting out such disturbing lines as, 'The little girl you dangled on your knee without mishap/Stirs something in your memory and something in your lap' and 'The kissing cousins slip outside to cuddle and confess'. He even manages to cram the word 'taramasalata' into the song, though, unusually, he uses it as a destination and not as the Greek meze that it actually is.

Related Tracks

'Tomorrow's (Just Another Day)' (with Madness) (Carl Smyth, Mike Barson)

Guest lead vocal on Madness single, February 1983.

'I had known (Madness) since they first recorded for Two-Tone', Elvis wrote in the 2004 liner notes for *Goodbye Cruel World*. 'They were now well into their phenomenal run of success on Stiff Records.' Indeed, Madness had achieved fourteen top 20 UK singles between 1979 and 1982 (plus their only US Top 10 single, 'Our House') before Elvis hooked up with them. 'Tomorrow's (Just Another Day)' was released as a double A-side with 'Madness (Is All In The Mind)'. Elvis was invited to sing lead vocals on a re-recording of the song, though he later lamented that 'my decision to perform the vocal in the style of Anthony Newley, may have been ill-advised'. Released on the 12' version, 'Tomorrow's (Just Another Day)' peaked at number 8 in the UK.

This song was released on the 2004 double-disc reissue of *Goodbye Cruel World* (Elvis reasoned that the song, 'illustrating a streak of melancholy that runs through their later work', suited the equally bleak lyrics of that album), though it was recorded before sessions for *Punch the Clock* commenced in late 1982; hence, the track appears here instead of in the *Goodbye Cruel World* chapter.

'Heathen Town' (Elvis Costello)

B-side of 'Everyday I Write The Book', 1 July 1983.

Elvis later expressed regret over the omission of 'Heathen Town' from *Punch the Clock*, explaining that even after the album was pressed, he was planning on substituting 'Love Went Mad' with this track. In the end, the right decisions were made: *Punch the Clock* was presented as a mostly upbeat album, and if 'Heathen Town' – a largely mid-tempo ballad – had appeared instead of the far perkier 'Love Went Mad', that balance would have shifted drastically. Written as an answer to Gram Parson's 1969 song, 'Sin City', there's not much here to save 'Heathen Town' from being one of the slighter tracks to have come from the *Punch the Clock* sessions.Its use as a B-side to 'Everyday I Write The Book' was the right choice.

'Night Time' (Paddy Chambers)

B-side of 'Everyday I Write The Book', 1 July 1983.

Not the more popular Ray Charles tune (which is titled 'Night Time (Is the Right Time)') but a more obscure song first released in 1966 by The Escorts, 'Night Time' was recorded during the February 1982 sessions that produced 'I Turn Around', 'From Head To Toe', 'The World Of Broken Hearts' and 'Really Mystified'. With a hard-working Steve Nieve providing not only the piano but also vibraphone and synthesized horn blasts, the song features prominent guitar and a drum sound that would resurface (to greater effect) on *Punch the Clock*. Suitably, 'Night Time' was later issued as the B-side of 'Everyday I Write The Book' in July 1983.

'The Flirting Kind' (Elvis Costello)

B-side of 'Let Them All Talk', 2 September 1983.

Like he did with 'Heathen Town', Elvis later lamented not including 'The Flirting Kind' on *Punch the Clock*, though his sentiments are a little more justified here. 'The Flirting Kind' is a fine track, dominated by a hard-working Steve Nieve on keyboards, Pete Thomas offering up a simple drum pattern (punctuated by congas, though they should be mixed a little higher), and Bruce Thomas exploring the higher range of his bass guitars. Deemed surplus to requirements, 'The Flirting Kind' eventually snuck out as the B-side to 'Let Them All Talk'.

Goodbye Cruel World (1984)

Personnel:
Elvis Costello: vocals, guitar, anvil
Maurice Worm: Random Racket
Pete Thomas: drums
Bruce Thomas: bass guitar
Additional personnel:
Gary Barnacle: saxes and electric sax
Jim Paterson: trombone
Luis Jardim: percussion
Daryl Hall: vocals on 'The Only Flame In Town'
Green: vocals on 'I Wanna Be Loved'
Recorded at SARM West Studios, London, February 1984
Produced by Clive Langer and Alan Winstanley
UK release date: 18 June 1984; US release date: June 1984
Highest chart places: UK: 10, US: 35
Running time: 44:18

'Congratulations!', the liner notes of the 1995 CD reissue of this album self-deprecatingly smirked. 'You've just purchased our worst album.' Elvis has been relatively unkind to *Goodbye Cruel World* since its release in June 1984, often treating it as the outcast of his many albums issued before and since. 'At least', he clarifies in the self-penned liners, 'that is the impression I've given over the years, and I am sure you could find many people who would agree with me'.

Elvis later explained that the period immediately following the release of *Punch the Clock* and its supporting tours was relatively harmonious, but his mood started to sour as the year wound down. By the time it was time to think about a new album, he took stock of the songs he had written and demoed, and summarized his frame of mind aptly: 'It seems I wasn't exactly in a cheerful and optimistic mood when I made this album'. It doesn't take a detective to figure out that songs with titles like 'Home Truth', 'Love Field' and 'I Wanna Be Loved' aren't going to be the easiest songs to listen to.

Acknowledging that much of the success of *Punch the Clock* was due to its production, Elvis asked Clive Langer and Alan Winstanley to return for a follow-up. But the songs he had written didn't lend themselves to the 'building block' method that Langer and Winstanley preferred. Elvis had hoped to record the album live in the studio, which was how he and The Attractions often got the best results, but Langer later admitted that 'he would have been better off going back to Nick Lowe. I wanted to carry on from where we had got to with 'Everyday I Write The Book', but Elvis was saying he wanted it really rough. I didn't think it was his greatest bunch of songs anyway, and we did say, 'It would be great if you could write some more pop songs'. But he never did'. Still determined to make the relationship, Elvis let his production team focus on shaping the singles ('The Only Flame In Town' and 'I Wanna Be Loved') while he had freer reign on the other eleven tracks. Elvis later wrote on his official website:

> I'd spent too much money on it to not release it, and I thought, on balance, the good things that I'd got wrong in the studio that were in the songwriting probably outweighed the bad things that I'd allow to happen in the production, which is not distracting anything from the effort that Clive Langer made to do the best. I mean, I announced to (Langer and Winstanley) that it was the last record I was ever going to make before we went in the studio. I decided to quit for all kinds of weird personal reasons ... I made Clive Langer's life impossible, and I take full responsibility for the failure of the production, 'cause I was asking them one time to do one thing and the next to do another, and changing my mind every fifteen minutes and driving everybody in the band mad. And really just getting it as wrong as you can in terms of the execution of what are basically a bunch of really good songs.

At the start of 1984, Elvis rented a room in F-Beat Records' office in Acton and, armed with a piano and a few guitars, began writing and recording demos of songs, almost as if he had taken a day job. If he wasn't feeling musically creative or felt that he became stuck on a particular phrase or verse, he would put paintbrush to canvas and create that way. (The crudely painted image on the inner sleeve – credited to Eamonn Singer and titled 'Pat and Mike' – was the result of one painting session.) However, the dark mood of the lyrics, combined with frustrating and tense sessions, made it abundantly clear that this was a less than harmonious period for Elvis. During the sessions, he and his wife finally parted for good, though their divorce had been a long time coming. 'I made *Goodbye Cruel World* and I was having a miserable time – I was getting divorced – and I basically ran away to sea and went off on a solo tour. I had a ball. It was my first time as a professional, but I'd done it a lot in my apprenticeship, as it were. I always enjoyed it. I did songs one night and then never again. The American leg was particularly great.' Elvis' first solo tour – which lasted throughout all of April 1984 – helped boost his self-esteem and gave him a chance to road-test his new material.

A squawking saxophone blast heralded the album before settling into a sound that wanted to recapture the refreshingly bright pop of *Punch the Clock* but failed. There are some moments of inspiration scattered throughout – the painfully honest 'Home Truth', the scorching 'Deportees Club', the now-obligatory protest solo record, 'Peace In Our Time', and the shimmering 'Love Field' – but the band sound like they are sleepwalking throughout, while Elvis sounds unsure of, and disconnected from, the material. The album attracted some positive reviews (*Melody Maker*: '(Has a) very taking-care-of-business air about it, a grave, serious urgency'; *Sounds:* 'Sad, depressing, but brilliant'), but it charted poorly, reaching 10 in the UK and 35 in the US, while the three singles – 'Peace In Our Time', 'I Wanna Be Loved' and 'The Only Flame In Town' – varied in success: 'I Wanna Be Loved' peaked at a respectable 25, while 'The Only Flame In Town', with guest vocals from Daryl Hall, struggled to 71.

Elvis and The Attractions took the album out on the road in May 1984, and it turned out to be a bittersweet experience for all involved. During his solo tour in April, Elvis had teamed up with T-Bone Burnett for some shows, discovering a musical ally who was performing the kind of material that was closer to Elvis' heart than what he had been working on with The Attractions. The two developed an alluring chemistry while on the road and began drafting up production ideas and pie-in-the-sky musician line-ups for an album they had yet to record.

Just as quickly as he had written and recorded *Goodbye Cruel World*, Elvis preferred to forget it. Having spent his time on the road solo, reclaiming the disappointing and sterile studio arrangements, with vibrant, stark, and compelling acoustic treatments, he was in no mood to play the game and promote the album by the record company's rules. Also, he was in love with The Pogues' bassist, Cait O'Riordan, and between that and his musical awakening, his confidence was on the rebound. It was now time for him to throw it all away and start from scratch.

'The Only Flame In Town' (Elvis Costello)

A-side, 18 August 1984; Peak position: 71

And, with a discordant squawk of saxophone and tick-tock drum machine, so begins *Goodbye Cruel World*, Elvis' much-maligned ninth studio album. The gloss is laid on pretty thick for 'The Only Flame In Town', with layers upon layers of synthesizer, Synclavier and drum programming that effectively buries The Attractions deep in a muddled mix. 'Ah well', Elvis mused later, 'it all seemed like a good idea at the time'.

Originally composed with Aaron Neville in mind, the song started as a minor key ballad, with Elvis and The Attractions laying down a superb rendition in rehearsals (available on the now-deleted 2004 double-disc CD reissue of *Goodbye Cruel World*, as is a solo live rendition that was closer to Elvis's vision). However superior this rendition may have been to the familiar album version, it was simply not single material, and with Elvis wanting to replicate the success of *Punch the Clock*, Clive Langer and Alan Winstanley suggested a new arrangement with some contemporary touches.

It didn't matter anyway because the tarted-up version wasn't a hit single either, despite the presence of Daryl Hall on vocal harmonies (Hall's presence was at the request of Elvis, who had become 'tired of hearing my own voice harmonizing with myself'). Released in August 1984 as the second single from *Goodbye Cruel World*, the song struggled to number 71 in the UK, though it was a minor hit in the US, peaking at 56 in the *Billboard* Hot 100 and 44 in the same magazine's Mainstream Rock chart.

'Home Truth' (Elvis Costello)

Clive Langer had suggested Elvis leave this song off *Goodbye Cruel World*, feeling that it was far too personal. But Elvis insisted, calling it, 'as stark, unguarded, and unpolished a lyric as I had written to this point. I could not find any disguise for the simple recitation of falling out of love with someone that I'd adored for many years'. After the bubblegum-pop confection of 'The Only Flame In Town' – a sombre lyric set to an upbeat arrangement – 'Home Truth' is a shock, with its downbeat 6/8 time signature and the sad lyrics of a relationship long past its disintegration point. Elvis meant business: *Goodbye Cruel World* wasn't going to retread the previous album's bright and breezy declarations of wedded bliss.

'Room With No Number' (Elvis Costello)

Sounding like an updated, uptempo version of 'Motel Matches', 'Room With No Number' is one of the jauntier songs on *Goodbye Cruel World*, with Elvis sounding engaged, and The Attractions springing to life – Bruce and Pete even get brief solos midway through the song. However, the story of illicit affairs taking place in a sleazy motel is obscured, due to the production featuring overbearing, trick-shot drums and synthesizers galore, so that it makes repeated listening laborious.

'Inch By Inch' (Elvis Costello)

Beginning life as 'Little Goody Two Shoes' during the *Imperial Bedroom* sessions, 'Inch By Inch' is a peculiar song on a peculiar album, sounding like the theme to a film noir in which the detective meets a damsel in distress. (Perhaps an update to 'Watching The Detectives'?). Curiously, the song borrows the bass line from The Beatles' 'I'm Only Sleeping' – referenced in the line, 'I just woke up from dreaming, I think' – the dreamy, almost sleepy arrangement further reinforcing the surreal atmosphere.

'Worthless Thing' (Elvis Costello)

One of the few upbeat songs on *Goodbye Cruel World*, 'Worthless Thing' at first pass sounds like a harsh put-down of a female companion – especially considering the personal nature of the album's first four songs – but it's actually a criticism of the media, specifically MTV and sensationalist journalism: 'Keep your hands off my life'. '(The song) was written when the mausoleum builders of the TV and magazine trade had only just started catching lightning and turning it into a museum piece', Elvis later wrote. 'It mentions a lot of things in passing: game shows, body snatchers, 'Elvis Presley Wine', obsessives, cable television, and 'an obituary... for every clockwork cat and conceivable kitten', but most of all it was about the lack of surprises. It is a pity that self-loathing wasn't more fashionable at the time.'

'Love Field' (Elvis Costello)

The second of four songs on *Goodbye Cruel World* to be written in 6/8 time, 'Love Field' is a slick ballad that 'sounded a bit like a Serge Gainsbourg production', according to Elvis. 'I even tried to make the words sound as if they had been badly translated from another language.' Chronicling the trajectory of a relationship, from its joyous start ('You lie so unfolded/In a love field/With your contempt for any modesty/In a love field') to its heartbreaking finish ('In a crooked house where things can be arranged/You're different from the rest/But you don't know how you've changed'), 'Love Field' is a triumph all 'round – especially the arrangement, with The Attractions turning in a superb performance, unadorned by many of the contemporary production techniques found elsewhere on the album.

'I Wanna Be Loved' (Farnell Jenkins)

A-side, 16 June 1984; Peak position: 25

In its original 1973 recording by Teacher's Edition, 'I Wanna Be Loved' was a sweet and sultry soul-infused plea for acceptance and love. In the hands of Elvis, The Attractions, and contemporary production, the song became bland, sterile, and boring. Jerky drum machine, a throaty saxophone, and heavily echoed vocals do not a hit Elvis Costello record make, though it would go on to be his highest UK chart placement since 'Pills And Soap', reaching 25 in the UK, but failing to chart at all in the US.

'The Comedians' (Elvis Costello)

B-side of 'The Only Flame In Town', 18 August 1984.

Later rewritten and given to Roy Orbison for his 1988 comeback album, *Mystery Girl*, 'The Comedians' is an average pop song in 5/4 time (with a shift to 6/8 in the chorus for good measure) that takes a general shot at temptation without committing to a side. As a result, the song is forgettable, and Elvis later lamented the 'bizarre arrangement, which drained any drama out of the song'. Instead, seek out his re-recorded demo circa 1987, specifically for Orbison, on the (now deleted) double-disc CD reissue of *All This Useless Beauty*, where he transforms the song into a tortured, heartbroken lament – or better yet, check out the stunning performance from the *Roy Orbison and Friends: Black and White Night* TV special.

'Joe Porterhouse' (Elvis Costello)

Written about 'the funeral of a family strong man', according to the 1995 CD reissue liner notes: '(I wanted) a name that would sound strong, a name with muscles, something to do with meat', 'Joe Porterhouse' is a rewrite of '(I Love You) When You Sleep': a track that Elvis gave to Tracie, who took the single to number 59 in the UK. Beefed up with a muscular backing and topped with keyboard flourishes reminiscent of 'You Little Fool', 'Joe Porterhouse' is thick with musical qualities, though the lyrical side seems a bit overdone.

'Sour Milk Cow Blues' (Elvis Costello)

'Sleepy' John Estes wrote a song called 'Milk Cow Blues', which Elvis Presley released as his third single in 1954. Similarly, Elvis Costello wrote an update called 'Sour Milk Cow Blues', though the result is largely underwhelming. Bursting with sequencer, synthesizers and loud drums, the song is brought down by indifferent words (the woman in the song is much more interested in her coffee than her man), though Elvis manages to sneak in some raw guitar licks among the din. Too little, too late.

'The Great Unknown' (Elvis Costello, Clive Langer)

After the successful first collaboration of Elvis and Clive Langer on 'Shipbuilding', another seemed inevitable. With music by Langer and words by Elvis, the song lacks the impact of the previous collaboration, though the lyrical premise is clever: the song is 'a fantasy about burying the title characters of various songs that have been repeated to the point of cliché'. The characters in question are Danny Boy in the first verse, Delilah (the biblical character, though the Tom Jones character is also referenced) in the second verse, and that other Elvis in the third, all meeting unfortunate ends. The premise is more interesting than the song as a whole which is largely forgettable.

'The Deportees Club' (Elvis Costello)

In a surprising and rare flash of inspiration, the penultimate track on *Goodbye Cruel World* is a loud, brash, and thrilling rock song. With a set of lyrics that are effectively a mini-epic whose story is far too convoluted to decipher properly, Elvis spits out the words with a loud precision, occasionally jumbling them here and there but retreating to whoops and screeches when impassioned enough. His wordplay is as sharp as ever here, particularly on the lines, 'How I wish that she was mine/I could have been a king in 6/8 time', though Elvis' own mental state is most obviously reflected in 'Schnapps, Chianti, Porter, and Ouzo/Pernod, vodka, Sambuca, I love you so', which concludes the performance uneasily, swirling into oblivion as the song comes to an indefinite conclusion.

To show that they hadn't merely been sleepwalking throughout the entire album, The Attractions are in fine form, with each member getting his turn to shine, be it Pete's devastating drum performance, Bruce's leonine bass rumble, or Steve's uncontrollable whirl around the keyboards. Gary Barnacle and Jim Paterson lend some much-needed menace on saxophone and trombone, respectively, creating a terse atmosphere that would later be revisited (almost as a theme) on *Blood & Chocolate*.

'Peace In Our Time' (Elvis Costello)

A-side, April 1984; Peak position: 48

The Imposter strikes again. Having managed to get an oblique political lambasting against Margaret Thatcher – 'Pills And Soap' – into the UK top 20 in 1983, Elvis tried again the following year with 'Peace In Our Time': a sombre, melancholy plea for the attainment of worldwide peace, and an end to nuclear threat. Performed almost exclusively by Elvis – with additional keyboards by Steve and trombone by Jim Paterson – the song is superbly sung and performed, though its naïvety, somewhat oblique lyric and decidedly radio-unfriendly arrangement, prevented it from being a hit single. The single, backed with a cover of Richard and Linda Thompson's 'Withered and Died', stalled at 48 in the UK charts upon its release in April 1984.

Related Tracks

'Withered And Died' (Richard Thompson)

B-side of 'Peace In Our Time', April 1984.

First recorded by Richard and Linda Thompson for their excellent 1974 album, *I Want to See the Bright Lights Tonight*, 'Withered And Died' was performed just once during Elvis' 1984 solo tour, but it was recorded during sessions for *Goodbye Cruel World* with just Elvis, on voice and guitar. This recording is sublime and poignant, with Elvis almost on the verge of emotional breakdown, most convincingly on the 'My dreams have withered and died' tag at the end of each verse. The song was issued as the B-side of The Imposter's 'Peace In Our Time' in April 1984.

'Turning The Town Red' (Elvis Costello)

B-side of 'I Wanna Be Loved', 16 June 1984.

Just to show that he was still capable of being a superb pop songwriter, albeit unconsciously, Elvis penned 'Turning The Town Red' as the opening theme song for Alan Bleasdale's comedy series, *Scully*, which ran on Channel 4 from 14 May to 25 June 1984. The song was an outtake from the *Goodbye Cruel World* sessions (recorded at Sarm Studios, with vocal and guitar overdubs at AIR Studios with Jon Jacobs co-producing), though was not written for the album, unsurprisingly, considering the throwaway, almost jokey lyrics, completely at odds with the rest of the album's material. Elvis explained that the premise of the series was 'the title character (dreaming) of leading out the Liverpool football team in front of their most dedicated fans on the Kop terrace. I also made a supporting appearance in the story as a nearly mute member of the central family, who is obsessed with railway timetables'.

Not wanting to let a good song go to waste, 'Turning The Town Red' was issued as the B-side of 'I Wanna Be Loved' in June 1984, though Elvis credited the single as a double A-side in the 1994 liner notes of *Goodbye Cruel World*. He's not wrong, just slightly mistaken: 'Turning The Town Red' was a double A-side on 12' vinyl releases of 'I Wanna Be Loved' in the UK, New Zealand and Australia, but was the B-side on all other issues.

'Baby It's You' (Burt Bacharach, Mack David, Barney Williams)

B-side of Nick Lowe's 'L.A.F.S. (Love At First Sight)' June 1984.

Recorded a month before *Goodbye Cruel World* was released, this cover of Burt Bacharach's 'Baby It's You' was recorded as a joint duet between Elvis and Nick

Lowe at Am-Pro Studios in London. First recorded by The Shirelles in 1961 but later made famous by The Beatles on their 1963 sophomore album, *With the Beatles*, it's the latter version that inspired this re-recording, drawing heavily from the laid-back vocals and musical delivery. Though the song is of little consequence, it's still a lovely performance, with Elvis and Nick duetting perfectly.

Much to Elvis's chagrin, Columbia Records refused to release the single because, 'according to them, it was 'too good', and they feared it would distract from both artists' current single releases.' Instead, the song appeared as a bonus track on Lowe's 'L.A.F.S. (Love at First Sight)' 12' vinyl single, and later on Elvis and The Attractions' 'The Only Flame In Town.' Most surprisingly, Elvis elected not to reprise 'Baby It's You' in performance when he joined up with its songwriter in 1998, though he would sing a few introductory lines from behind the curtain before the first song.

'Walking On Thin Ice' (Yoko Ono)

Released on the various artists' compilation, Every Man Has a Woman, September 1984.

While on the Clocking On Across America tour during the summer of 1983, Elvis was invited by Yoko Ono to meet with her in New York City for a potential contribution to a collection of her own songs as recorded by other artists. The resulting album, *Every Man Has a Woman*, featured Harry Nilsson, Rosanne Cash, and even Yoko's son, Sean. Elvis and The Attractions contributed a rendition of 'Walking On Thin Ice': the very song that Yoko and her husband, John Lennon, had been working on the night of his senseless murder. Elvis later claimed that ' (Though) I would not pretend that her records are exactly a fixture on my turntable, I was happy to help complete one of her husband's last projects, which one must imagine was conceived out of love'.

Because the band were hard at work on tour at the time, and there was little time to jump into a studio and record the song in a familiar setting, two options were given; to record in either Memphis or New Orleans. Yoko's people contacted both Willie Mitchell and Allen Toussaint, respectively, to produce the session, and before long, Elvis, The Attractions, and the TKO Horns were under the guidance of Toussaint at Sea Saint Studios in New Orleans. This would mark the first (though not the last) time that Elvis would work with Toussaint, and the result was interesting, to say the least: heavily distorted vocals from Elvis and a fairly insistent backing became monotonous after a while, though the TKO Horns added their own flourishes to liven up the song.

'Really Mystified' (Tony Crane, Johnny Gustafson)

Released on the various artists' compilation, *Sometimes a Great Notion*, November 1984.

Recorded at the same sessions as 'From Head To Toe', 'The World Of Broken Hearts', 'Night Time' and the initially unreleased, 'I Turn Around' (which later turned up on the 1994 and 2002 CD reissues of *Imperial Bedroom*), The Merseybeats' 'Really Mystified' is another superb cover that Elvis later mistakenly recollected as being 'in our repertoire since our first London club dates'. (It was actually performed only once, on 16 December 1977.) Regardless, the song was deemed surplus to requirements and languished unreleased for two years before sneaking out on the charity album, *Sometimes a Great Notion*: compiled by Rupert Hine for the British Deaf Association.

King of America (1986)

Personnel:
Little Hands of Concrete: vocals, acoustic and electric guitars, mandolin
Additional personnel:
T-Bone Burnett: guitars, backing vocals
Mitchell Froom: organ, harpsichord, doctored piano
T-Bone Wolk: electric guitar, piano accordion, electric bass
Jerry Scheff: string bass, electric bass
Mickey Curry: brushes, drums, sticks
Michael Blair: marimba
James Burton: electric guitar, dobro, acoustic guitar
Tom Canning: piano
Ralph Carney: saxophone
Jim Keltner: sticks, drums, brushes
Earl Palmer: brushes, drums
Ron Tutt: brushes, drums
Ray Brown: double bass on 'Eisenhower Blues'
David Hidalgo: harmony vocal on 'Lovable'
Jo-El Sonnier: French accordion on 'American Without Tears'
Steve Nieve: piano, organ on 'Jack Of All Parades' and 'Suit Of Lights'
Pete Thomas: drums, sticks on 'Suit Of Lights'
Bruce Thomas: bass guitar on 'Suit Of Lights'
Recorded at Ocean Way, Sunset Sound, and Sound Factory Studios, Hollywood, July-October 1985.
Produced by the Coward Brothers.
UK release date: 21 February 1986; US release date: February 1986
Highest chart places: UK: 11, US: 39
Running time: 58:04

The genesis of Elvis' first true solo album can be traced as far back as 1981 when his extramarital affairs had landed him in trouble with his wife. Though she ultimately forgave his indiscretions, they both knew that the marriage was on life support; still, he attempted to woo her back with the *Almost Blue* album and unofficially dedicated it to her. She was a huge fan of C&W music and had even introduced Elvis to most of the C&W music he had covered.

In 1984, with the disharmonious sessions for *Goodbye Cruel World* yielding an unsatisfactory result, Elvis fell into a deep depression. Not only was he drinking heavily, he was also dispirited with where his career was going. Additionally, with a cloud of indifference and hostility (depending on the member) surrounding The Attractions at the time, Elvis seriously considered scrapping the album and recording it all again on his own, but he simply couldn't afford to do so. In order to recoup some of the financial and creative losses, Elvis went out on a solo world tour in the spring and winter of 1984, stripping down the new songs to their bare essentials, performing them as intended.

During the tour, Elvis gained a mutual alliance in support act, T-Bone Burnett: a Texan singer/songwriter promoting his newly-released *Proof Through the Night* album. A mutual appreciation and almost brotherly rapport developed between the two, and eventually, they were appearing during each others' sets as part of a joke partnership that eventually morphed into the Coward Brothers. Elvis and Burnett traded ideas offstage, with the latter suggesting that the former record his next album with the voice and acoustic guitar as the main attraction. After a series of exploratory sessions throughout 1985 – with one of them resulting in the only Coward Brothers single to date ('The People's Limousine' b/w 'They'll Never Take Her Love Away From Me') – Elvis finally decided he'd collected enough material for his new album, and recording began in earnest that July.

Another significant partnership that had developed by this time was with The Pogues: a rough-and-raw Irish band whose original name, Pogue Mahone, translates from Irish to English as 'kiss my arse.' Elvis was keen to discover new music, and friend, musician, and record store employee, Philip Chevron, couldn't recommend the band highly enough. Elvis checked them out at the Diorama in Euston on 22 June 1984 and became immediately enamoured – not just with their music but also with their strikingly intense bassist, Cait O'Riordan. Seemingly under the guise of being an appreciator of their music, an enthralled Elvis asked the band if they would like to support him on tour with The Attractions that autumn (indeed, he and Chevron would produce their critically-acclaimed *Rum Sodomy & the Lash* album the following year), but he really just wanted to get to know Cait better. As their relationship blossomed, however, Elvis and Cait would estrange themselves from both their bands.

Despite experiencing a romantic and professional renaissance, Elvis made sure his dance card wasn't too overwhelmed in 1985; it had become all too clear that the frantic and exhausting schedule of the previous eight years had to stop. Elvis and The Attractions only show of the year was at the Miner's Strike Benefit Concert at the University of London on 9 March, where they kicked off their set with the searing Margaret Thatcher indictment, 'Betrayal' (released four years later as 'Tramp The Dirt Down'), while he made a handful of live guest appearances (Ricky Skaggs, John Hiatt, Los Lobos and The Pogues) which periodically interrupted a quick nine-date Pacific Rim tour with T-Bone Burnett. (Elvis also made a solo appearance at Live Aid, performing 'All You Need Is Love'.) The year may have been one of relative inactivity in terms of live performances, though under cover of L.A.'s famous Sunset Sound Studios, he was busy crafting one of his most honest and personal albums ever.

Going in the complete opposite direction to his previous two records, Elvis 'started thinking more about the songs and much less about the records. It became clear to me that I had to write very, very simple songs. It just seemed a lot easier for me to say something straight out'. This meshed well with Burnett's insistence that Elvis concentrate more on the voice than on creating a sonic wall of noise. Suitably, Elvis asked his new friend to produce the sessions, along with noted Los Angeles producer Larry Hirsch.

The first order of business was to pick musicians for the album. Elvis had decided to record half of the material with The Attractions, and the other half with session musicians of his and Burnett's choosing: these included Ron Tutt on drums, Jerry Scheff on bass, and James Burton on guitar, all of whom had played in Elvis Presley's Taking Care of Business (TCB) Band in the 1970s. The primary function of this quartet (with Elvis sarcastically credited on acoustic guitar and vocals as 'The Little Hands of Concrete', after a comment Nick Lowe made about Elvis' guitar playing years prior) was to record the slower ballads, though a portent of Elvis' changing moods came on the first day of sessions when he and the assembled band ran through four takes of 'Our Little Angel' before a satisfactory version had been achieved; then, to liven up proceedings, an unscripted performance of 'The Big Light' – a bawdy, raucous roller coaster of a tune – was called. The result was so much to Elvis' liking that the first take remained the only one, and it promptly secured a well-deserved spot on the album. After limbering up, the assembled band once again cooled down with an emotional reading of 'American Without Tears'.

The following day, Tutt, Burton, and Scheff recorded 'Glitter Gulch', 'Lovable', 'Indoor Fireworks', and the outtake 'Shoes Without Heels', though only the first recording was deemed usable. With the early sessions out of the way and with Elvis feeling more comfortable with the material, the next round began, this time with entirely different musicians: Tom Canning on piano, Mitchell Froom on Hammond organ, Ray Brown on upright bass and Earl Palmer on drums. This new line-up recorded 'Poisoned Rose' and 'Eisenhower Blues'. During the recording of 'Poisoned Rose' with this legendary set of musicians, Elvis' nerves got the better of him, though once a successful take was captured, Burnett cued up 'Eisenhower Blues' to let the band loosen up a bit. ('When T-Bone had pencilled these names next to studio dates, somewhere over the Pacific, it had seemed like a brilliant idea', Elvis later wrote. 'It had never been my intention to hire off-the-peg 'legends' for the hell of it.') Unfortunately, Elvis' excessive whiskey consumption after the session was so considerable that the following day's session was nearly cancelled. Though he was able to prop himself up and – with Burton and Scheff from the first round back on their respective instruments, Froom retained from the second round, and newcomers Jim Keltner on drums and Los Lobo frontman David Hidalgo on harmony vocals – cut the final versions of 'Indoor Fireworks', 'Lovable', 'I'll Wear It Proudly', 'Sleep Of The Just', 'Little Palaces', and the outtake, 'King Of Confidence'.

With most of the record now complete, and Elvis enjoying himself more than he had in a while, it came time to record with The Attractions: a prospect that neither side seemed to be looking forward to. In The Attractions' defence, they had been summoned to Los Angeles while Elvis was still working with the other musicians and had spent most of their time waiting for his call. Already disenchanted with being cast aside so callously, the band's mood soured. 'By the time The Attractions arrived in Hollywood, there was more than half an album's worth of material in the can', Elvis later wrote. 'This meant that our sessions had a doomed air of suspicion and resentment. After spending so much time together on the road, T-Bone and I had a rapport based on rumour that unwittingly drove a wedge between the band and myself.' Elvis and The Attractions ran through six songs – 'Brilliant Mistake', 'Blue Chair', 'Next Time Round', 'Baby's Got A Brand New Hairdo', 'Betrayal', and 'Suit Of Lights' – with the intent that all of them wind up on the album, 'so that the contrast of accompaniments would be heard to best effect'. However, the sessions yielded only one usable recording ('Suit Of Lights'), and Elvis was disappointed that The Attractions were unable to complete a satisfactory take of 'Brilliant Mistake', which he had designed to be the album opener and had felt was best suited to The Attractions. 'Alas, nothing else seemed to fall into place', he later wrote, 'and the recording schedule had to move on. This left my sullen and estranged band hanging around our hotel, harbouring a grudge or honing an embittered anecdote'.

Bruce Thomas – the Attraction with the biggest grudge to harbour – later said, 'I thought, 'If you're going to fire us, fire us'. It was like being sacked by instalments'. He also noticed, with some dry amusement, that Elvis' hotel room had become festooned with the singer's portrait from the album sleeve photo sessions. While Elvis later reasoned, with some muted hostility, that he was doing this only to pick the right image to represent the cover, Bruce attributed it to Elvis' growing megalomania and identity crisis. 'I stuck a Burger King crown on my copy.'

The other Attractions were in no better a mood than the bassist. While Pete Thomas remained mostly friendly throughout Elvis' estrangement from The Attractions, he still fumed at the unprofessional manner in which Elvis dealt with the situation: 'I was furious about it, absolutely furious. He should just have said, 'I'm going to make a solo album, don't worry about it'. The worst thing about it was that we were all there, day after day, not getting the call to go into the studio'. Meanwhile, Steve Nieve was in the midst of a nervous breakdown that would last until 1987, when Elvis finally put the band out of its misery.

It seems fitting that the one song featuring The Attractions was also the epitaph to his stage name: emboldened by his creative and romantic rebirth, and recognising that he had done all he could do as Elvis Costello, Elvis legally reverted to his given name, adding Aloysius as a lighthearted tribute to comedian, Tony Hancock. Tellingly, Elvis has never released an album under his given name; in fact, Columbia Records was nonplussed by Elvis' decision, and when he insisted it go out as D. P. A. MacManus, they refused. The uneasy compromise was the unwieldy 'The Costello Show Featuring The Attractions and The Confederates'.

This wasn't the first instance of record company interference: midway through the sessions, record label executives who had heard some of the playbacks, demanded more radio-friendly songs. Having deluded themselves into believing Elvis was poised to deliver another *Armed Forces* and 'Oliver's Army', the collection of whiskey-soaked country ballads sent them into a panic, and they insisted he come up with some more commercial material. One of the last songs cut for the album was a cover of The Animals' 'Don't Let Me Be Misunderstood', recorded after recovering from a bout of laryngitis and not delivered with the utmost of confidence or enthusiasm. Regardless, Columbia was placated, and on 21 February 1986, *King of America* was released to glowing reviews. But this didn't translate to sales, and the album stalled at number 11 in the UK (his first album since the debut to miss the UK top 10) and 39 in the US, a fairly common chart placement for his albums of late.

'Brilliant Mistake' (Declan MacManus)

Kicking off *King of America* with a lovely upright bass intro and brushed drums is 'Brilliant Mistake', a song which Elvis half-jokingly referred to as 'the session's theme song'. With its poetic verses, an outsider's view of America in the early 1980s – 'where they pour Coca-Cola just like vintage wine' – the song gallops along at a mid-tempo pace, occasionally switching narrative and even becoming more personal as it goes on. The second verse deals with a dimwitted reporter working for the ABC news ('It was as much of the alphabet as she knew how to use'), while the third verse recalls Elvis' description of his 'ever-changing impressions of America': dashed dreams, consumerism, and tricks done with mirrors and chemicals.

The introductory line gave the album its name, which Elvis particularly relished, saying that some of the songs on the album continued 'the theme of exile and a simultaneous attraction and repulsion to an ideal. That is why the album is called *King of America*. It is inherently contradictory'.

'Lovable' (Declan MacManus, Cait O'Riordan)

After the weighty intro, a little lightweight relief was necessary. While 'Lovable' might seem a little 'too' lightweight to sit on an album primarily full of sobering ballads, the energy in the performance more than justifies its inclusion. Elvis wrote the song with Cait O'Riordan during one of their first writing sessions, and it's a fine expression of joyous love that the two were surely feeling at the time. They had only been in a relationship for a few months by this time, but it was a much-needed shot in the arm for Elvis after the dispiriting marital events that had inspired *Goodbye Cruel World* (and, in fact, much of *King of America*).

'Our Little Angel' (Declan MacManus)

The first song recorded for *King of America* – in July 1985 – 'Our Little Angel' also had the distinction of featuring members of Elvis Presley's famed backing band, The TCB Band (James Burton, lead guitar; Jerry Scheff, bass; Ron Tutt, drums), and what a lovely song to kick off the sessions in earnest. 'Our Little

Angel' is a delicate country ballad, with Elvis' intimately pleading vocal – affecting an involuntary twang at times – telling the story of a lovelorn woman left at the altar one time too many ('In a white dress she wears like a question mark'), and a well-meaning man doing his best to get on her good side ('You're the marshmallow valentine that got stuck on her clothes', 'You're never the bridegroom, she's always the bride').

'Don't Let Me Be Misunderstood' (Bennie Benjamin, Sol Marcus, Gloria Caldwell)

A-side, 24 January 1986; Peak position: 33

After a perfunctory run-through of a rough assemblage of the new album, the Columbia Records executives weren't impressed and noted a severe lack of singles. Elvis, less than pleased with the record label intervention, conceded to the suggestion and recorded a few more upbeat songs, among them a cover of 'Don't Let Me Be Misunderstood', first made famous by Nina Simone and then by The Animals in 1964.

Elvis' rendition is, like many of his latter-day covers, perfunctory if disposable; the most interesting aspects being the prominent use of marimba (performed by Michael Blair), and Elvis' raspy vocal: the result of too much drinking, and the salt-kissed sea air of Los Angeles wreaking havoc on his voice. At the time, some critics and fans made the baseless accusation that Elvis was ripping off Tom Waits – who was then enjoying a critical, if not commercial, renaissance with his album, *Rain Dogs* – but if Waits was upset, he never let on: later in 1986, he would serve as the emcee at Elvis and The Attractions' date at Los Angeles' Beverly Theater.

So was Columbia's hand-wringing worth it? 'Don't Let Me Be Misunderstood' – backed with the *Goodbye Cruel World* outtake, 'Get Yourself Another Fool' – continued the infuriating tradition of a cover out-performing an Elvis original in the charts, peaking at 33. Columbia was pleased, but Elvis wasn't: sensing an overreach in their commercial decisions, he would ensure that he had the final say in which singles would be released from his next album.

'Glitter Gulch' (Declan MacManus)

Elvis returned to his favourite societal punching bag – television – on 'Glitter Gulch', an update of 'Worthless Thing' from *Goodbye Cruel World.* This time it's 'the tale of a game show swindle', with the beautiful but sharp-tongued host, Madam X, and the show's impatient, diminutive ringleader. Elvis later wrote that the song was written after witnessing 'some of the grotesques that I had encountered on my own American travels'.

'Indoor Fireworks' (Declan MacManus)

Coming as close as he ever would to a public apology for the way his marriage disintegrated, 'Indoor Fireworks' paints a depressing picture of what life must have been like in the Costello household at the time: 'Everybody loves a happy ending, but we don't even try/We go straight past pretending to the part where everybody loves to cry'. The fireworks in this case, weren't those of romance but of marital dispute and arguments.

Recorded fairly early on in the sessions, the vocal track was laid down the day after the particularly joyous celebration of nailing the challenging 'Poisoned Rose' in a minimum of takes. As Elvis explained, 'I arrived for the next day's session in pretty poor shape ... Only shaking slightly, I took up my position, and after one complete take, we had 'Indoor Fireworks'. Naturally, we always went on to record several further attempts, just in case there was any temptation to take the easy way out. It was probably best that we cut it quickly, as this kind of romantic obituary is not something you would want to labour over'.

Nick Lowe returned the favour that Elvis and The Attractions had done him in 1978 by covering 'Indoor Fireworks' on his 1985 album, *The Rose of England*. Elvis later explained that he envisioned the song as a cowboy ballad but that most true cowboys would have baulked at the lines, 'You were the spice of life/ The gin in my vermouth'. Apparently, real cowboys don't drink gin.

'Little Palaces' (Declan MacManus)

Elsewhere on *King of America*, Elvis muses on the joys of the New World, despite the country's many shortcomings. However, he didn't hold back his disdain at the then-current socioeconomic politics of Britain, on 'Little Palaces', a stark and chilling tirade, as venomous as 'Pills And Soap' was sinister, or 'Shipbuilding' was mournful. Calling it 'as close to a folk song form as I had ever used', Elvis sounds positively Dylan-esque as he spits out the vitriolic words, railing against the mundanity of Britain and the prevalence of domestic violence. The song is set to a minor key acoustic guitar melody, performed deftly by Elvis, who later overdubbed a scratchy mandolin.

'I'll Wear It Proudly' (Declan MacManus)

Having eulogised his first marriage in 'Indoor Fireworks', Elvis now celebrates his blossoming relationship with Pogues bassist Cait O'Riordan, on 'I'll Wear It Proudly': a song 'about the danger and uncertainty of desire'. He also gets in a few digs at certain members of The Pogues ('I'll wear it proudly through the dives and the dance halls/If you'll wear it proudly through the snake pits and catcalls'), who considered Elvis an interloper, disrupting their inter-band harmony: while Elvis and Cait were off on their own, lost in the honeymoon phase of a flourishing romance, the others would taunt him behind his back. Before long, they became bold enough to do it to his face. Unsurprisingly, this only hastened Cait's resignation from the band.

'American Without Tears' (Declan MacManus)

Recorded on the first day of the *King of America* sessions, 'American Without Tears' (its title inspired by Terence Rattigan's 1936 play, *French Without Tears*) was based on 'a chance meeting with a couple of former G.I. brides during a tour of Florida', Elvis later explained. 'They had volunteered their stories while I was drinking at an adjacent table. The names and locations were changed, but it stayed pretty true to their tale of exile and escape. It is as close as this record comes to having a theme.'

Elvis wasn't quite done with the characters in this song, returning to them the following year on the 'Blue Chair' B-side 'American Without Tears No. 2 (Twilight Version)'.

'Eisenhower Blues' (J. B. Lenoir)

Following the wistful celebration of American life and culture in 'American Without Tears', is a reading of J. B. Lenoir's 'Eisenhower Blues': a lament over the politics and economic downfalls during Ike's presidency. That original recording was so controversial that Lenoir's record company insisted he instead release it as 'Tax Paying Blues'. Recorded in April 1954 and released shortly thereafter as the B-side of 'I'm In Korea', the song has a charming humour that is retained in Elvis' recording, even if it's the most disposable song on *King of America*.

'Poisoned Rose' (Declan MacManus)

Recorded on the same day as the rollicking 'Eisenhower Blues', 'Poisoned Rose' is one of the most poignant and stunning songs about the end of a relationship that Elvis had yet written. Opening with his naked, exposed voice – backed up only by Ray Brown's deft upright bass work – the intro proved difficult for Elvis to nail successfully. Upon finally achieving a satisfactory result: 'Cue the celebration and crack open the Glenlivet!'. The plaudits were entirely justified, for 'Poisoned Rose' undoubtedly possesses the album's finest vocal.

'The Big Light' (Declan MacManus)

Recorded on the first day of the *King of America* sessions, 'The Big Light' wasn't intended to be recorded with The TCB Band – Elvis preferring the trio for any country-styled ballads. But, nailing 'Our Little Angel' in only four takes called for the addition of this 'fast, grim comedy that was written in the awful wake of a drunken solo acoustic demo session earlier that year'. It's not the album's most significant performance, but it speaks volumes to anyone who's ever indulged in a little too much 'inspiration', as Elvis put it, and has had to face the consequences the next day.

Johnny Cash, with his own well-known 'inspiration'-inspired consequences, recorded a cover of the song that would open his 1987 album *Johnny Cash Is Coming to Town*.

'Jack Of All Parades' (Declan MacManus)

This 'unapologetic companion to 'I'll Wear It Proudly'' perfectly sums up Elvis' romantic 1985 rebirth, as well as the equally meaningful decision to revert to his given name. Having destroyed his first marriage as 'Elvis Costello', he was determined to become 'Declan MacManus' again and to not make the same mistakes this time around. (As time would tell, the third time proved to be the charm.)

'Jack Of All Parades' was one of the earliest songs Elvis wrote for *King of America* and was inspired by his blossoming relationship with Cait O'Riordan. Biographer Graeme Thomson, in his excellent book, *Complicated Shadows*, credits Cait with shaking Elvis from his post-divorce doldrums and serving as a valiant muse for most of the album – and beyond. It's hard to disagree: both 'Jack Of All Parades' and 'I'll Wear It Proudly' are unabashed love songs that feature some of Elvis' most beautiful, painful, and revealing lyrics. He wouldn't allow himself to be this vulnerable again until 2003's *North*.

'Suit Of Lights' (Declan MacManus)

Pity the poor Attractions – their future with Elvis was looking dimmer and dimmer as the *Goodbye Cruel World* tour wore on. Yet despite informing them at the tour's conclusion that their services were no longer required, Elvis still envisioned *King of America* as a half-Attractions/half hand-picked musicians album. In the summer of 1985, Steve, Bruce, and Pete reported for duty in Los Angeles, but even the best-laid plans have a way of working out differently sometimes, and Elvis was pleased to discover that eleven of the songs that would turn up on the album were completed within the first three days of recording.

So where did that leave The Attractions? Mostly in their hotel rooms, waiting for the call that came too late. 'This meant that our sessions had a doomed air of suspicion and resentment', Elvis later wrote. The singer's newfound kinship with T-Bone Burnett was yet another nail in the band's coffin, and the camaraderie between the two didn't include Elvis' increasingly estranged band. 'In these circumstances, I suppose it is hardly surprising that (they) delivered some of their worst-ever performances.'

As a result, only one recording, 'Suit of Lights', was deemed salvageable: the sole performance where the band is playing as if their lives depend on it. As such, it's no coincidence that it's one of the best performances on the album. Here, Elvis sings of the death of Elvis Costello and the rebirth of Declan Patrick Aloysius MacManus: the body being pulled out of the cold, cold ground and dressed up in a suit of lights. There's little lament here – more a celebration as if Elvis was unloading a heavy burden. Note also the switch of personage, something that Elvis often did: in the first verse, '‹He' went to work that night and wasted 'his' breath'; and in the final verse, 'I went to work that night and wasted 'my' breath'.

'Sleep Of The Just' (Declan MacManus)

King of America closes on a bleak note with this cautionary tale of sibling hypocrisy. As Elvis explained at the time, 'It's just about a soldier whose sister is a porno model, and he's standing there all proud and full of himself in his uniform and looking down on her, and all the time, it's her picture that's up on the barracks wall'. She also has a checkered past, having been assaulted by soldiers who 'even looked like her brother in the army but she never mentions him', while her brother is busy rhythmically admiring the centrefold of a dirty magazine, blissfully unaware that the girl is, in fact, his sister. He's proud of his career choice yet condemns his sister for what she does, while she is equally condemning of his military career, considering her unsavoury experience with soldiers.

Instead of setting the story to a sleazy, sinister arrangement, Elvis opted for a sympathetic, mournful melody, which frames the characters as what they are: flawed humans. Despite the sombre and unsettling manner in which *King of America* concludes, 'Sleep Of The Just' is still a fine song and is a true testament to Elvis' songwriting talents.

Related Tracks

'The People's Limousine' (as The Coward Brothers) (Henry and Howard Coward)

A-side, 20 July 1985.

The first recorded work of The Coward Brothers to be released, 'The People's Limousine' was written by Elvis (Howard) and T-Bone Burnett (Henry, his birth-name) 'during a long and occasionally surreal journey through Italy' in 1984. The two started performing it live shortly thereafter, and it has endured since, often showing up whenever the Brothers' paths crossed.

The song was recorded in February 1985 at Sunset Sound and the Sound Factory, with a line-up of Howard and Henry on vocals and guitars, David Miner on bass, and Ron Tutt on drums. Released as a single in July 1985 – a week after Elvis' Live Aid appearance, the single predictably failed to attract much attention, mostly because no one had any idea who The Coward Brothers actually were!

'They'll Never Take Her Love From Me' (as The Coward Brothers) (Leon Payne)

B-side of 'The People's Limousine', 20 July 1985.

This B-side of 'The People's Limousine' is a serviceable rendition of the Leon Payne C&W weeper. However, with competition from other versions by the likes of Hank Williams, George Jones, Emmylou Harris, and John Prine (whose own recording was released the following year), the Coward Brothers version paled in comparison. This choice as B-side is curious, as it hadn't been performed live yet; in fact, its first performance (in Auckland, New Zealand) wouldn't be until a month before its release, and its second – and to date, final – performance wouldn't be until 11 June 2009 in Vienna, Virginia (Incidentally, a concert this author attended).

'Baby's Got A Brand New Hairdo' (Declan MacManus)

B-side of 'Don't Let Me Be Misunderstood', 24 January 1986.

One of six Attractions recordings from their fractious *King of America* sessions, 'Baby's Got A Brand New Hairdo' is a slight if enthusiastic recording, with Elvis testing the upper regions of his vocal cords, as The Attractions thrash away at a manic pace behind him. Steve's keyboards are practically doing battle with Elvis, while Bruce's guttural bass rumble interlocks with Pete's frantic yet rock-steady drumming. Recorded live in the studio on 21 August 1985, Elvis was later dismissive of the song: 'Groovy title. Shame about the song. The one redeeming moment is after the line, 'She looks like Billy Boy Arnold saying 'I wish you would'' when Bruce quotes the riff'.

'Get Yourself Another Fool' (Frank Hollywood, Ernest Tucker)

B-side of 'Don't Let Me Be Misunderstood', 24 January 1986.

Recorded by Sam Cooke in 1963, 'Get Yourself Another Fool' was recorded by Elvis and the Attractions in October 1984, at the same session as the first version of 'I Hope You're Happy Now'. Intended for the B-side of that song – before Elvis had a change of heart (see the song's entry in the next chapter) – this is a sublime performance and didn't deserve to be wasted as the B-side of 'Don't Let Me Be Misunderstood'.

Blood & Chocolate (1986)

Personnel:
Napoleon Dynamite: vocals, guitar; effects on 'Home Is Anywhere You Hang Your Head'; Vox Continental organ on 'Honey, Are You Straight Or Are You Blind?'; harmonium on 'Battered Old Bird'; additional bass, tambourine on 'Poor Napoleon'
Steve Nieve: piano, organ; harmonium on 'Battered Old Bird'
Pete Thomas: drums
Bruce Thomas: bass guitar
Additional personnel:
Nick Lowe: acoustic guitar on 'Home Is Anywhere You Hang Your Head', 'I Want You', 'Honey, Are You Straight Or Are You Blind?', 'Blue Chair' and 'Next Time Round'
Cait O'Riordan: vocals on 'Crimes Of Paris' and 'Poor Napoleon'
Recorded at Olympic Studios, London, March-May 1986.
Produced by Nick Lowe with Colin Fairley
UK release date: 15 September 1986; US release date: September 1986
Highest chart places: UK: 16, US: 84
Running time: 47:55

'There is not an awful lot that needs explaining about this record', Elvis wrote in 1995. 'It's a rock 'n' roll record with a couple of weird ballads and few pop songs thrown in ... The terrible experience of The Attractions' (*King of America*) Hollywood sessions was far from forgotten. There was a good chance that this was going to be our last work together.'

After the stark beauty and frailty of *King of America*, Elvis decided it was time to write something that was louder and brasher, combining the frenetic energy of *Get Happy!!* with the simmering tension of *This Year's Model* and *Armed Forces*. This shift wasn't so much a creative decision as it was a reaction against his record company: an indifferent Columbia Records wasn't keen on *King of America*, which Elvis couldn't help but take personally. Believing that Columbia wanted the long-overdue spiritual successor to *Armed Forces*, he set about writing some of his most sinister and paranoid lyrics to date while, perversely (and much to his label's frustration) stripping away as much nuance as possible, writing in the 2002 CD reissue liner notes:

> I had written most of the songs very quickly using a 1930s Gibson Century acoustic guitar that had an attractively clanky sound but provided little invitation to intricate harmony or melody. When 'Honey, Are You Straight Or Are You Blind?' came to me in a dream, I had to capture it on a cassette player with just the accompaniment of my slapping on the kitchen counter, as there was no guitar on hand. These were not songs that you had to worry about.

Recognising that these songs required the simmering tension of his erstwhile and estranged former bandmates, Elvis placed a call to each of The Attractions

and then approached Nick Lowe to produce the sessions. (Roger Bechirian – by this point an in-demand producer – was working with the reformed Monkees on their reunion album *Pool It!*; Colin Fairley served as co-producer instead.) With everyone on board, an initial session was held in February 1986 at Eden Studios to record, with Jimmy Cliff, 'Seven Day Weekend': Elvis's forgettable contribution to the equally forgettable comedy film, *Club Paradise*. While the sessions went better than expected, when they started work on the album the following month at the famed Olympic Studios, the 'air of suspicion and resentment still lingered', according to Elvis. Lowe later recalled in a March 1992 *BBC Radio One* documentary that 'it was a much more uptight situation. It wasn't a gang feeling. I never really knew what their internal arguments were, but they had plenty of that, Lord knows'.

Because of the underlying resentments, Elvis and Lowe 'agreed to an approach that would get the music recorded before the band and I fell out completely'. At Olympic Studios, Elvis especially favoured the live room: 'Big enough for a full orchestra, so we filled it with our live monitor system and played at something approaching stage volume. Although it is commonly thought that high volume in the studio creates an uncontrollable sonic picture, this approach seemed to suit the material entirely'.

Songs were captured within the first three or four takes (most being first passes), not only because of the relative simplicity of the material but mostly because of the volatile relations between Elvis and the band. Bruce Thomas later said of the recording method: 'It was a total mess. There were no screens, no separation on the drums, the bass, nothing. It was a soup ... (Elvis) created situations where you just basically wanted to strangle the bastard. You'd be just about to walk out and he'd say, 'What's the problem? What's wrong?'. So you'd stay and do the take and he'd get the angst that he wanted, but then you'd go away for two days thinking, 'Fucking bastard'. I suppose it was an artistic device, and maybe I can now see it a lot more than I did at the time'.

Songs could be easily separated into two categories: the kind of masterful pop/rock that Columbia had wanted ('I Hope You're Happy Now', 'Blue Chair', 'Next Time Round' and 'Crimes Of Paris'), and tuneless, primal rants (essentially everything else). The only times these categories crossed paths were on the masterful and raw ballads, 'Home Is Anywhere You Hang Your Head' and 'Battered Old Bird', which came as close to a declaration of love and nostalgia, respectively, as Elvis would get on the album. '(This) was a pissed-off 32-year-old divorcé's version of the musical blueprint with which I had begun my recording career with The Attractions', Elvis later wrote. 'Having said all of this, the year I made this record was also the year of my marriage to Cait O'Riordan. There were a lot of things that I wouldn't have to do again. Like messing up my life just so I could write stupid little songs about it.'

The first 'stupid little song' to be released from the sessions was the deliberately uncommercial and unrepentant 'Tokyo Storm Warning', split into halves for the 7' release. Despite the glaringly obvious singles, 'I Hope You're

Happy Now' and 'Blue Chair', Columbia finally gave in and let Elvis have his artistic statement. Elvis believed that 'Tokyo Storm Warning' was a hit (he had a history of giving the average single buyer's attention span too much credit) and was furious when it wasn't, so he dug his heels in deeper and issued 'I Want You' as the follow-up.

Wrapped in a crimson/red sleeve with a dementedly sinister painting by Elvis' artistic alter ego, Eamonn Singer, and credits written in Esperanto, *Blood & Chocolate* was released in September 1986, only seven months after *King of America*. (A limited edition cassette version – released only in the UK – was wrapped in a cellophane sleeve that vaguely resembled a Cadbury's Bournville chocolate bar, but this was withdrawn after complaints from the candy company.) The album performed somewhat admirably (16) in the UK, but it limped to 84 in the US. By this point, an exasperated Columbia no longer had any clue what to do with Elvis. He charged that the label 'hated it and subsequently just fucking buried it'.

Having released two albums in the same year – and wanting to perform both live – Elvis considered 'hiring' certain bands (Los Lobos, ZZ Top and The Heartbreakers were mooted, though, tellingly, not The Attractions) to back him up, depending on the material, for a pay-per-view event, but this wasn't remotely feasible. Instead, Elvis would block-book a series of theatre dates in major cities and then present a different show each night, with five possible shows in all. The first night was Elvis with The Attractions, performing a rather predictable 'greatest hits' set; the second night, Elvis performed solo, with T-Bone Burnett joining midway through for a Coward Brothers set and an *ad hoc* band dubbed The Confederates (James Burton, Jerry Scheff, Jim Keltner and Mitchell Froom) joining for the encore; the third night, The Confederates got a whole show to themselves, with most of *King of America* performed along with rootsy, good-time Americana and rock'n'roll; the fourth night was a wildly original idea called The Spectacular Spinning Songbook; and the fifth night was a towering, rarities-laden set with The Attractions – the kind of presentation that was expected of Elvis and his band.

It was the Spectacular Spinning Songbook nights that rightly attracted the most attention. Elvis' concept was a pretty daring spectacle, especially for him: a massive game-show-inspired wheel covered with song titles would be spun by members of the audience selected by the emcee: Napoleon Dynamite (Elvis doing his best P. T. Barnum schtick) – or any other celebrity who happened to passing through town – and whatever song was chosen would have to be played. There were 38 choices in all, ranging from his best-known single and album tracks to forgotten B-sides and obscure or bizarre covers, such as Prince's 'Pop Life' or ABBA's 'Knowing Me, Knowing You'. (In some events, Elvis would deliberately 'fix' the wheel, depending on how long the show was dragging on.) After the audience member's spin, they could then either be shown to the Society Lounge, where they could listen to the song on stage while enjoying a non-alcoholic refreshment or dance along to the song in a go-go cage. 'Our experience suggests that the world is full of frustrated gogo dancers', Elvis later quipped.

The tour reviews were almost unanimously positive, with many critics commending Elvis for his eclecticism and ability to engage a crowd. The musicianship of all the bands was also praised, though many found that The Confederates suffered because they came across more like session musicians than a band, which meant that The Attractions' sets were almost always held in higher regard. However, Elvis' solo sets were by far the most intimate, with the structure often shaped by his mood in the particular moment. He gave song characters backstories, sang impromptu a cappella standards, and even introduced short spoken-word pieces into his set: 'How Joe Soap Got Into Everyone' and 'Getting Into Showbiz' were both pointed reactions to Bruce Thomas, who had begun writing a memoir of his life on the road, published four years later as the dreary *The Big Wheel*.

The tour had to be streamlined for the European and UK dates – The Confederates got the axe for budgetary reasons – and, with Elvis, Cait O'Riordan, and The Attractions being the only survivors, tempers flared once again. Certain Attractions members viewed Cait as a Yoko Ono figure, and while she had stopped by the occasional *Blood & Chocolate* session (contributing backing vocals to 'Crimes Of Paris' and 'Poor Napoleon') and had been received cordially if coolly, her constant presence – and Elvis' obvious preference towards her – splintered the band beyond repair. At the tour's end in December, Elvis took the band out to dinner and told them he couldn't afford their salaries any further and that the band was effectively broken up. As he explained in a March 1992 *BBC Radio One* documentary,

> We were never particularly friendly. We didn't spend lots of time together when we weren't on the road. We were thrown together so much because we were touring, so you assumed there was a very strong bond. But what it really was, was me and a really great group. It had to be my decision the way we went because I was the mug out front.

The original intention was to send off The Attractions with a trio of dates at the Royal Albert Hall in January 1987. But, given the circumstances, nobody performed at their peak. (Perhaps Elvis should have waited until after these shows to have told them of his decision.) They got a second chance to make a final impression later that year, at the Glastonbury Festival on 20 June: Elvis played a seventeen-song solo set, deliberately prolonging bringing on The Attractions until the last possible second. But when they appeared, they were given eleven songs to make their statement, and they didn't waste a single precious moment. The set started with 'I Hope You're Happy Now' and focused mostly on live favourites ('Oliver's Army', 'You Belong To Me', 'Watching the Detectives', '(What's So Funny 'Bout) Peace, Love And Understanding?'; some rare covers being either complete performances ('Knowing Me, Knowing You',

'Leave My Kitten Alone') or interpolations into originals ('Day Tripper' in 'I Hope You're Happy Now', 'Twist And Shout' in 'Less Than Zero', 'Down By the River' in 'Watching the Detectives'). For the final song, the band tore into 'Poor Napoleon', creating a sonic soup of noise while Elvis wailed lines from 'Instant Karma!' and 'Like A Rolling Stone'. 'I'm sure it was supposed to mean something at the time', he later mused. The band unplugged, walked off the stage, and that was it. The Attractions were no more.

'Uncomplicated' (Declan MacManus)

A twangy Telecaster riff that leads into an unrelenting and savage aural beating of drums, bass, and choppy organ, is the most appropriate of introductions to a record that Elvis has called 'a pissed-off 32-year-old divorcé's version of *This Year's Model*'. This is obvious in his vocal delivery of 'Uncomplicated', which mixes an uncomfortable combination of love with disgust and revenge, as Elvis howls about an unfaithful woman. The title of the album is given away in the first line, conjuring up images of a battered old bird holding a box of chocolates, returning to her abusive lover for what is presumably not the last time. It's fitting that the next song is 'I Hope You're Happy Now'.

It's no coincidence that Elvis' first deliberate rock album in years kicks off with a song called 'Uncomplicated', but he later posited that he may have subconsciously been writing a kiss-off to The Attractions ('You think it's over now/But we've only just begun'): 'I don't know whether to some extent I was writing the band's story'.

'I Hope You're Happy Now' (Elvis Costello)

B-side of 'I Want You', 7 November 1986.

It took four separate attempts spread over 18 months before Elvis finally got the desired arrangement of this song, a venomous sendoff to an ex-lover. (Who Elvis was narrowing his crosshairs in on is anyone's guess.) The first attempt – recorded with The Attractions in October 1984 at Eden Studios – was delivered with perhaps a bit 'too' much venom. It was initially intended as a stand-alone single release before that idea was shelved, but the song was a live favourite at the time, with Elvis and The Attractions even performing it on *The Tonight Show* the month before its recording.

Blaming the arrangement, Elvis returned to it the following February as he recorded solo demos for *King of America*, this time approaching the lyrics with a mournful, almost regretful tinge. Figuring he'd nailed it this time, he brought it to the sessions that July, recording a tastefully restrained C&W rendition with Jim Keltner, Jerry Scheff, and Mitchell Froom; this too, didn't make the cut, and Elvis shelved the song. While recording *Blood & Chocolate* the following spring, he realised the sonic soup he, Nick Lowe, and The Attractions had concocted, suited the song perfectly: 'Time had lent the song a little humour to lighten its originally murderous intent', Elvis later wrote. 'Now it almost sounded like pop music.'

As for the other versions, they all eventually saw release: Elvis's solo recording was issued first, as the B-side of 'I Want You', that November, while the *King of America* recording was erroneously included on the 2003 *Singles Volume 3* box set instead of the correct version. The first Attractions recording was later issued as a bonus track on the 2004 *Goodbye Cruel World* CD reissue.

'Tokyo Storm Warning' (Declan MacManus, Cait O'Riordan)

A-side, 22 August 1986; Peak position: 73

This epic and tenacious Centrepoint of *Blood & Chocolate* was written following a particularly hellacious transcontinental flight from 'Narita to Heysel via Pompeii, Port Stanley, Paris, and London', as Elvis later explained. 'Fatigue can play cruel tricks upon your perceptions, but arriving early one violent morning, among the frenzied commuters, with the storm clouds down beneath the tops of the tallest building, Tokyo 'did' seem like the setting for a particularly brutal science-fiction story (perhaps something by Philip K. Dick). So thinking, 'Why stop there, let's trash the world', I recalled twenty years of nightmares, actual or altered, to present this thug's-eye-view of the planet.'

Captured in one continuous take – the first, according to Elvis – with vocal overdubs and fixes added afterwards (a clearly hoarse Elvis, at around the six-minute mark, was left unaltered, though some reverb was added to the happy accident), 'Tokyo Storm Warning' was the longest song to be recorded and released on an Elvis and The Attractions album. That record would be broken two songs later on the same album, with 'I Want You', but only by 17 seconds.

Still smarting from Columbia's indifference – and their lack of confidence in his ability to deliver a hit single – Elvis insisted that 'Tokyo Storm Warning' be the lead single from the album. And while his label could have easily insisted on 'Blue Chair' or 'I Hope You're Happy Now' instead, they gave in to his obstinacy, and the song – sliced approximately in half and spread out over both single sides (the 12' presents the full version and is backed by the *Trust* outtake, 'Black Sails In the Sunset') – was released three weeks ahead of the album. The single stalled at number 73 in the UK, and Elvis blamed Columbia. As punishment for them, he decided the follow-up single would be the even less chart-friendly 'I Want You'.

'Home Is Anywhere You Hang Your Head' (Declan MacManus)

Nestled between the manic 'Tokyo Storm Warning' and the psychotic 'I Want You', is this poignant self-lament ('Here comes Mr. Misery'), with the narrator taking stock of himself in the mirror after another embarrassing public breakdown. Whether drawn from personal experience or by taking some creative liberties, 'Home Is Anywhere You Hang Your Head' is a pretty succinct summation of Elvis' mental state since his messy divorce and romantic redemption with Cait O'Riordan.

He later wrote that the song started life with a brighter, poppier melody, but that it didn't fit the 'tale of a man driven mad by love', so, 'I placed it in an almost impossibly low register, which made me sound as if I was either seething or gasping for breath: 'Method singing', I suppose. This was backed by a droning accompaniment and features some fine bass-playing from Bruce in the coda, as accordions and spoons fly past his window'. (Hence then, the baffling Esperanto credits of 'Balgo, Kanoj, Klingovaroj' to Napoleon Dynamite.)

'I Want You' (Declan MacManus)

A-side, 7 November 1986.

'The intimate, if not almost pornographic, tone of ... 'I Want You' (was) typical of my mood at the time', Elvis later wrote. The song starts off quietly, sounding like a ballad that could have fit on *King of America*, with only Elvis on vocal and Nick Lowe on acoustic guitar. Then, with the strike of the Telecaster, Elvis and The Attractions take the listener on a most harrowing journey.

The narrator is so consumed by his emotions and thoughts – love, lust, rage, jealousy, anger, bitterness, murder, desperation, poignancy, passion – that he can't seem to get the words out quick enough, repeating 'I want you' after each line, to drive home his point. The vocal performance – easily one of Elvis' best ever – conjures up images of a deranged madman, imagining his obsession with her new lover, plotting something vicious or malicious, if only he could get a moment alone with her.

The song, recorded in the first take, comes to an uncertain close, achieved because Elvis felt 'that no matter how quietly the band had played, there seemed to be too much accompaniment in the last verse during playback. We fixed this by switching off the band, track by track until all you can hear at the end is what was bleeding onto my vocal mike'. Engineer Colin Fairley later praised the performance: 'The vocal performance sent shivers down my spine. The mix used on the album is the original monitor mix thirty minutes after we cut the track, warts and all. I'm convinced this performance from the whole band was achieved because of this unusual studio setup'.

This intense, unnerving, and frankly chilling song, was released as the second single from *Blood & Chocolate* in November 1986. While 'Tokyo Storm Warning' had eked into the UK charts at 73, 'I Want You' presented in its full six-minute-43-second glory, unsurprisingly failed to chart.

'Honey, Are You Straight Or Are You Blind?' (Declan MacManus)

Lasting just over two minutes and dominated mostly by thudding drums and Elvis' amateurish attempts on a Vox Continental organ, 'Honey, Are You Straight Or Are You Blind?' is a lively rock song that works well as the second-side opener. Even more titillating is the lyrical matter, which appears to be about a woman coming in between a couple, though the attraction is not between the new woman and the main character, but between his girlfriend and the new woman ('She's coming in between us, you know that she is/I'm not holding on to her but one of us is'). Amusing and lightweight, the song is a necessary chaser to the sheer intensity of side one.

'Blue Chair' (Declan MacManus)

A-side, 31 January 1987.

Opening with a lilting minor-key melody (borrowed from Prince's 'Manic Monday' and 'Raspberry Beret), 'Blue Chair' was salvaged from an unusable ('lacklustre', per Elvis' description) Attractions recording from the *King of America* sessions, and repurposed into something approaching a pop song. This arrangement suited the song best, combining the aggression of the Elvis of old with the chart awareness that pop-star-Elvis had learned from 'Everyday I Write The Book'. He even does a passable John Lennon impression as the bridge leads into the third verse.

While he could have had a hit single with The Attractions version, Elvis instead released the recording from the *King of America* sessions – with T-Bone Wolk on guitar and bass, Mickey Curry on drums, and Steve Nieve on keyboards – remixed at Eden Studios in January 1987, with additional vocal work taking place then. (The 2002 *Blood & Chocolate* reissue CD credits Mitchell Froom with organ, but the original single release doesn't.) This version pumped up the rhythm to a danceable groove, with multi-tracked Elvis providing doo-wop styled backing vocals. Most significantly, it sounded nothing like what Elvis would record for either *King of America* or *Blood & Chocolate*, instead sounding like a castoff from *Get Happy!!* or the 'From Head To Toe' sessions.

Backed with the sequel song, 'American Without Tears No. 2 (Twilight Version)' (the 12' vinyl added that song's predecessor and the *King of America* outtake, 'Shoes Without Heels'), 'Blue Chair' predictably failed to attract any attention, stalling at 94 in the UK.

'Battered Old Bird' (Declan MacManus)

While Elvis would often take events from his personal life and insert them into song, he rarely did the same with his childhood. It's surprising, then, that the cinematic 'Battered Old Bird' dug into the lives of 'the tenants of the house in which my family had a small basement flat until I was five years old'. The song chronicles the eccentricities of a group of miserable and lonely characters: the landlady's husband, two old maids, the mild man who 'chopped off the head of a visitor's child', the Macintosh man who keeps Christmas trees in a cupboard 'in case of emergencies', and finally, the little boy 'who's going to do big things'. All the characters were real, experienced by the young Declan, and left a profound impression on his imagination, though 'some of the more nightmarish characters have been distorted by time'.

A trio of drastically different versions of the song were recorded: the first was an uptempo rave-up that Elvis equated to the style of Johnny Allen – probably more as a lark to shake off the tension instead of as a serious attempt – while the second and third came closer to Elvis' vision. He preferred the majority of the second take but liked a particularly emotional delivery of the line 'Pieces of him are already scattered in the attic' from the third. Producer Nick Lowe was then tasked with making the two different versions make sense, doing so by 'joining (the) two contrasting performances together with a combination of vari-speeding and bold editing, using a smear of harmonium in the way a scene might dissolve in the movies'.

'Crimes Of Paris' (Declan MacManus)

Try to assemble the puzzle of a story within 'Crimes Of Paris', and you might find that the pieces don't all fit. But that's half the fun when you have such picturesque metaphors as 'You're tough and transparent as armoured glass' and 'As he crawled through the door/And poured out more of his creeping-Jesus heart'. And I've got a gold star for anyone who can tell me what 'I heard that you fell for the 'Hell or to Hammersmith Blues'' means.

The other half of the fun is noting all of the influences in the song, where Elvis throws one part The Kinks, one part glam-rock band, Slade, one part traditional folk song 'Wild Mountain Thyme', one part self-reference (Elvis' unreleased outtake, 'Suffering Face', from *King of America*), and a dash of Little Willie John's 'Leave My Kitten Alone' (also recorded during the sessions) into the blender, and comes up with this delightfully demented slice of pop/rock.

'Poor Napoleon' (Declan MacManus)

Elvis was succinct in his description of 'Poor Napoleon' – 'about a very raw affair' – and cast Cait O'Riordan as 'the voice of pity', moving the focus from what could have been one of his most aggressive and confrontational production tactics: the song 'was originally completely covered up in the sheets of white noise and feedback that can be heard briefly before the band's entrance', Elvis later wrote in the 2002 CD reissue liner notes. 'Little by little, I pulled it out in order to reveal the song in which a proud and vain character finds his love fatally compromised.'

'Poor Napoleon' is still darkly twisted and demented, mirrored suitably in the production, with each instrument bathed in echo and blending in to provide a murky soup. Sometimes an instrument will momentarily rise above the din – a Hammond B3 note here, the higher reaches of a Fender Precision bass there – and Elvis briefly competes with himself ('I dubbed on the instrumental duel between Hofner bass guitar and tambourine'), but this is not meant to be accessible pop-rock.

In June 1995, Elvis reclaimed the song at his acclaimed performance at the Meltdown Festival, where he and jazz guitarist, Bill Frisell, delivered a stunning rendition. Seven of the eight songs performed that night were included on the mini-album, *Deep Dead Blue*, released two months later.

'Next Time Round' (Declan MacManus)

Pissed off with Columbia Records and aware that relations within his band were approaching terminal decline, Elvis resuscitated 'Next Time Round' from the failed *King of America* sessions with The Attractions and turned it into an up-tempo rocker. Positioned deliberately as the album closer, it's no coincidence that this song of a failed relationship would become The Attractions' epitaph, though it's just as likely to be about Elvis' ex-wife, his ex-mistress, or Columbia Records themselves.

Related Tracks

'Seven Day Weekend' (Jimmy Cliff, Elvis Costello)

A-side with Jimmy Cliff, summer 1986.

This forgettable, if energetic, throwaway was commissioned for the equally forgettable comedy film, *Club Paradise*: a Robin Williams vehicle also starring Peter O'Toole, the always excellent Eugene Levy, and Jimmy Cliff (who co-wrote the song and duets with Elvis) as Williams' tax-evading friend. Recorded in February 1986 at Eden Studios, this session reunited Elvis with The Attractions after the acrimonious *King of America* sessions yielded unsatisfactory results. These sessions were successful enough to warrant a full-scale reunion; indeed, 'Seven Day Weekend' wouldn't cut the mustard as an album track, but it serves its purpose as a soundtrack song and even has some wild guitar work. At the very least, it's miles better than 'Party Party'.

Released as a single ahead of the film, 'Seven Day Weekend' (with Cliff receiving top billing), backed with Cliff's 'Brightest Star' (neither Elvis nor The Attractions were involved in the B-side), failed to chart.

'Black Sails In The Sunset' (Elvis Costello)

B-side of 'Tokyo Storm Warning', 22 August 1986.

An outtake from the *Trust* sessions, recorded at DJM Studios, 'Black Sails In The Sunset' is dominated mostly by piano and an over-busy drum pattern, as Elvis sings of a careless woman performing various misdeeds. (He later opined that it 'denoted a further disenchantment with the rewards of pop life', with a similar lyrical theme to 'New Lace Sleeves': 'The less attractive aspects of the triumph of supposedly civilized culture over instinct and passion – just yer usual pop song nonsense'.) Deemed surplus to requirements, the song was dusted off for the B-side of 'Tokyo Storm Warning' in August 1986.

'End Of The Rainbow' (Richard Thompson)

Released on the various artist's compilation, The Anti-Heroin Project: It's a Live-In World, November 1986.

Elvis had long been a fan of pioneering guitarist Richard Thompson, even hoping to have him contribute guitar to *Goodbye Cruel World*. Though that didn't pan out ('The notion never got as far as making the call'), Elvis nevertheless incorporated several of Thompson's songs into setlists on his first solo tour and recorded 'Withered and Died' during sessions for *Goodbye Cruel World*. Another song from the terrific *I Want to See the Bright Lights Tonight* album was 'End Of The Rainbow', a feature of Elvis' solo live set in 1984, though 'not necessarily to the delight of audiences across the world'. When asked to contribute a song to the double-disc charity LP, *The Anti-Heroin Project: It's a Live-In World* (with contributions from the likes of Ringo Starr, Bonnie Tyler, Paul McCartney, Eurythmics, Dire Straits and Wham!), Elvis recorded this Thompson song. Unfortunately, this recording was 'utterly ruined by unauthorised overdubs': a bass guitar and harmony vocal laid over Elvis' stark acoustic guitar and vocal.

Still feeling that the song should not have gone unheard, Elvis recorded it again on 21 July 1985 during the *King of America* sessions, maintaining the subtleties of his original performance in the stripped-back acoustic guitar/vocal arrangement, even though it ultimately failed to make the album.

'American Without Tears No. 2 (Twilight Version)' (Declan MacManus)

B-side of 'Blue Chair', 31 January 1987.

Preferring to keep his characters confined to one song instead of running loose around his catalogue, Elvis rarely dabbled in sequels but couldn't help himself with 'American Without Tears' and Arnie LaFlamme: 'It's a very worrying thing when you find that somebody you thought you had created in your imagination, packs his suitcase and leaves for Venezuela', he quipped as he introduced the song during a 1986 concert. 'This is exactly what happened to me. I wrote this song called 'American Without Tears', about two English ladies that I met, and I wrote this story about – the next thing I know, the husband of one of the ladies packed his suitcase and moved to Venezuela. So I thought I would go down there and catch up with him and see what the hell he thought he was doing.'

Recorded during the mixing session for the 'Blue Chair' single at Eden Studios in January 1987, the song features Elvis on all instruments (including bass guitar and the less conventional celeste, marimba, and harmonica: which replaces the wistful accordion on the original), and was tucked away as the B-side of that single, and also released on the *Out of Our Idiot* compilation that same year.

'Shoes Without Heels' (Declan MacManus)

B-side of 'Blue Chair', 31 January 1987.

This *King of America* outtake was recorded with The TCB Band (James Burton, Jerry Scheff, and Ron Tutt) and is a pleasant enough track, though Elvis recognised its weaknesses ('written in ten minutes on the back of a hotel cocktail napkin'), noting that it 'sounds as if we might have been running out of luck by (the end of the sessions)'. Despite its gentle country shuffle and an extended Burton guitar solo, the song was left off the album and instead was issued as the B-side of 'Blue Chair'. start here

'A Town Called Big Nothing (Really Big Nothing)' (Declan MacManus)
'Return to Big Nothing' (Declan MacManus)

A and B-side, 4 May 1987.

This interesting, if inconsequential, contribution to Alex Cox's film, *Straight to Hell*, was commissioned by the director after Elvis wandered onto the set and landed a role as a butler named Hives, 'toting a pump-action shotgun'. The Pogues had been cast as 'a family of teetotal, nonsmoking, coffee-addicted desperados', according to Elvis, who was only there to visit Cait O'Riordan. Opening with more than 90 seconds of Spanish motif acoustic guitar and acoustic bass, the song was written and recorded during filming in Spain and features a stripped-back group of musicians: Pete switched on the drum machine, then added percussion and tambourine; Steve – credited as Steve Hart on the sleeve – played piano; Elvis' father Ross played trumpet and added flamenco claps; Cait and Elvis sang the fairground vocals; and Elvis himself played everything else and added the whispers. Sy Richardson – one of The Pogues' rivals in the film – narrated the song: 'The story that (Sy) tells, has nothing to do with the movie', Elvis later wrote in the 1995 CD reissue: 'in fact, it probably has more plot than *Straight to Hell*! On the other hand, I would not say that I wrote this with an entirely straight face'.

Released in May 1987, credited to The MacManus Gang, and backed with a superfluous remix ('Return To Big Nothing'), the single predictably failed to chart.

Postscript: This Is Only the Beginning

After Glastonbury on 20 June 1987, Elvis made himself scarce: he was in no rush to get back into the recording studio or onto a stage. For the first time in over a decade, he had time to himself again, he had neither a band nor a record contract, and he had never felt freer. Holed up in Dublin with Cait O'Riordan, Elvis could come and go as he pleased without being bothered too much. When he felt inspired to write, he did so. He recorded few demos the rest of the year, preferring to enjoy his freedom. (The former Attractions weren't so lucky as to be able to relax, and all dove into session work, with Steve Nieve also leading the house band on *The Last Resort with Jonathan Ross*.)

But Elvis didn't rest for too long, for he had some important writing to do. Paul McCartney had started the decade with the esoteric new wave pastiche, 'Coming Up', and two years later, the stellar *Tug of War* album. But a series of subpar releases (*Pipes of Peace*, *Press to Play*) and poor decisions (*Give My Regards to Broad Street*) meant that by 1987, his stock had never been lower. Needing a shot in the arm, he contacted Elvis and asked if he'd fancy writing some songs. Not wanting to be caught off-guard by McCartney, Elvis agreed, and brought two song fragments he had been working on: one a fairly forgettable pastiche rocker:'Pads, Paws And Claws', the other, a more substantial piece inspired by his paternal grandmother, Molly, though it was her confirmation name that provided the song with its title of 'Veronica'. McCartney brought 'Back On My Feet', and the two swapped ideas and suggestions, eventually coming up with their first legitimate co-write, 'The Lovers That Never Were'.

Inspired by working with the former Beatle, Elvis suggested another writing session later in the year. By the end of 1987, a further eight songs had been written and demoed, with Elvis claiming four of the songs for himself: 'Veronica' and 'Pads, Paws And Claws' for *Spike*; 'So Like Candy' and 'Playboy To A Man' for *Mighty Like a Rose*. McCartney got six: 'Back On My Feet' (B-side to 'Once Upon A Long Ago'); 'My Brave Face', 'You Want Her Too', 'Don't Be Careless Love' and 'That Day Is Done' for *Flowers In The Dirt, and* 'The Lovers That Never Were' for *Off the Ground.* Two remained unrecorded by either artist ('Tommy's Coming Home' and 'Twenty Fine Fingers'). The sessions were so productive that another three songs were written in December 1990: 'Mistress and Maid' for McCartney's *Off the Ground*; 'Shallow Grave' for Elvis' *All This Useless Beauty*, and 'I Don't Want To Confess', which remained unrecorded.

Elvis also helped McCartney produce his four *Flowers In the Dirt* co-writes, though he later diplomatically admitted that, 'I think we're better as a songwriting team than as co-producers'. He wasn't as charitable in conversation with Michel Lavidiere in 1998, sneering, 'Paul has a clever way of sidestepping confrontation by making jokes, like, 'Well, you can never trust anything he says because he hates effects!'. Rather than disagreeing with you, your argument is devalued before it's started. After a while, that made the production rather redundant'.

By February 1988, Elvis had collected enough songs that he felt compelled to start work on his first post-Attractions solo album. He also had the benefit of *carte blanche* with his new record company, Warner Bros. Now finding himself 'working with the budget of a small independent movie', Elvis 'had the blueprint of five albums in my head,' he wrote in the 2001 CD reissue of *Spike*. 'Having felt hostility turn into invisibility at Columbia, I offered Warner Bros. their choice. I would even shoot it out with a highly commercial producer if they so desired – believing the songs and my voice could hold their own. They told me to make whatever record I wanted. I seem to have elected to make all five albums at once'.

By far his most musically diverse album to date (it was recorded in four different cities: New Orleans, Dublin, Los Angeles, and London), *Spike* also contained little of the high-energy rock of The Attractions. But that didn't mean Elvis was done with his past entirely; his next project was envisioned as an Attractions project, and a series of exploratory sessions in 1990 eventually degraded into the same acrimony and resentment from three years prior. *Mighty Like a Rose* – released in 1991 – did find Pete Thomas working with Elvis again, meaning that at least one bridge had been rebuilt.

Emboldened by the success of 'Veronica' (his first – and to date, only – top 20 single on the *Billboard* Hot 100), and, to a lesser extent, *Spike* and *Mighty Like a Rose*, Elvis challenged his new record label with increasingly mature but arcane releases, like *The Juliet Letters* (recorded with The Brodsky Quartet and marking his commercial debut as a composer) and *Kojak Variety* (a covers album recorded in Bermuda and deliberately released five years later with little fanfare), before the long-delayed Attractions reunion happened in 1993.

While Elvis had made good with Pete, the other two were still not on speaking terms with their former boss. It wasn't until late 1992 when Elvis ran into Steve (at a session for Sam Moore, who was recording Elvis' 'Why Can't A Man Stand Alone?') that the two got talking again, and when Elvis began recording his next album – *Brutal Youth* – the following year, he called Steve to overdub some piano parts on some primitive exploratory recordings.

The only piece of the puzzle missing was Bruce Thomas, and Elvis wasn't ready to walk back over that bridge. The bassist had written a rather scathing takedown of life on the road in *Time Out* magazine (it opens with that classic first line, 'I farted and flung back the warm cocoon of bedding': on a par with 'Call me Ishmael' or 'Lolita, light of my life, fire of my loins'), eventually published in book form as *The Big Wheel*. Elvis was less than pleased with Bruce's depiction of him (he was referred to either as 'The Pod' or 'The Singer' and depicted as an overweight drunk with a sweating problem) and channelled his rage into song. 'How To Be Dumb' – released on *Mighty Like a Rose* – took aim at 'the funniest fucker in the world', where 'every fleeting thought is a pearl'.

It's no surprise, then, that Elvis drafted Nick Lowe as bassist for *Brutal Youth*, though some of Elvis' slower songs were too melodic for Lowe. Producer, Mitchell Froom, who had worked with Bruce on a Suzanne Vega album, suggested Elvis call Bruce. 'At first (he) hated the idea', Froom recalled. 'But I think he started thinking about it musically and then he came back and said, 'Maybe Bruce and I will get together and have a cup of tea or something. And just see'.' Froom called Bruce, who was also reluctant but warmed to it once he was told that Steve was on board. With the two parties now willing to talk to each other, Elvis made the first move, though his timing wasn't the best: 'He actually rang up in the middle of an earthquake in L.A.', Bruce later recalled. 'I said, 'Look, I do want to talk to you, but I'm in the middle of an earthquake at the moment!'. He was probably quite pleased to have had an impact.'

The Attractions were thus, reborn, in all but name: *Brutal Youth* was credited to Elvis Costello (not unfairly, as only five songs featured all band members), and he would introduce the musicians as 'these gentlemen up here on stage with me' on the supporting tour. But there was no mistaking that The Attractions were back in full force, and while the rough edges had been smoothed down over their seven-year hiatus, they still played as if their lives depended on it.

But Elvis wasn't keen on reforming The Attractions on a full-time basis: a smart move, considering that the old war wounds and tensions started to resurface during the recording of *All This Useless Beauty*, the only album credited to Elvis and The Attractions since their reformation. While Pete had always gotten along with Elvis, and Steve was now enjoying a renewed surge of creativity and a newfound respect from Elvis (the two would perform dates together throughout the United States in 1996, and again periodically thereafter), Bruce felt the same resentment he had bottled away all those years ago, starting to surface again. During the supporting tour for *All This Useless Beauty* (nicknamed the What Goes Around Comes Around tour, itself a pointed reference to the splintering relations), Bruce began to emotionally drift away again, and – due to friction with Cait O'Riordan and more frequent confrontations with Elvis – his playing suffered. In July 1996, after a backstage dressing down from Elvis, Bruce checked out: he decided then and there that he would never work with Elvis again, and it started to show in his playing, his body language and his attitude. Elvis' mood quickly soured too, and by the time the band reached the final stretch in Japan that September, the two hadn't spoken to each other in nearly a month. The final concert, in Nagoya, was bittersweet, though it did find The Attractions playing with a rejuvenated passion (probably because they were looking forward to it concluding more than anything). After the show, Bruce and Elvis shook hands, said their farewells ('Whenever', Bruce said; 'Yeah, whenever', Elvis responded), and again went their separate ways. 'You won't see them again', Elvis promised. 'I had a slight feeling of sadness on the last night that we played. It was like the last night of your childhood. I knew I wouldn't do that again. When somebody is deliberately fucking it up, you have to get rid of them. It's as simple as that.'

Elvis' mood on the tour was further soured by the realisation that Warner Bros. had no intention of promoting him or the new album. Elvis had few remaining friends at the label, and his increasingly radio-unfriendly songs weren't bringing in the numbers he needed. When they asked for a new song for a compilation album they had reserved $1,000 to promote, he baulked and gave them the two-fingered sendoff track, 'The Bridge I Burned', which had evolved from an impromptu line Elvis sang instead of the chorus of 'You Bowed Down' ('I should have never walked over that bridge I burned'), when relations had deteriorated entirely between him and Bruce.

Determined to not rush into a new record contract, Elvis essentially retreated from the rock world, instead writing an album with Burt Bacharach – the highly-acclaimed, *Painted From Memory*. This collaboration was long overdue: Elvis had long been a fan of Bacharach – covering 'I Just Don't Know What To Do With Myself' as far back as 1974 while still a member of Flip City – and had wanted to work with him for a long time. But it was musical supervisor Karyn Rachtman, who connected the two. She was presently working on the film *Grace of My Heart* and decided that a Costello/Bacharach composition was needed. Given the immediacy of the film world, the song needed to be completed yesterday, and a scrapped working session complicated an already tight timeline. Elvis was in the unenviable position of having to send his ideas via fax and telephone from Dublin to Bacharach in Los Angeles, but the elder songwriter loved what he had written. Before long, 'God Give Me Strength' was written (and debuted while The Attractions were still on good terms in 1995) and earned the pair a Grammy nomination. Elvis later wrote that 'to have written a song like 'God Give Me Strength' and simply stopped, would have been ridiculous, so about a year later, we began a series of writing sessions'.

Painted From Memory reinvigorated both Elvis and Bacharach's careers, and before long, Elvis was ready to return to the rock world and started writing some more visceral songs. But his new record label, Polygram, was merging with Universal, and he once again found his supporters there were either being let go or were jumping ship. Unwilling to get lost in the shuffle once again – and furious that Polygram hadn't promoted the album better – Elvis shelved a planned rock album for 1999, instead going on tour with Steve Nieve as a duo. With Bacharach already moving on to other projects, Steve was the next best thing, and he and Elvis further developed the musical bond they had rekindled in 1992.

By 2001, Elvis was ready to make a racket with a band again and contacted Steve and Pete about performing some live dates together. Their first appearance was at the Meltdown Festival in June 2001, while their proper live debut was on 15 July in Kilkenny, as support act for Bob Dylan. The former Attractions had lobbied to get Bruce back into the band, but Elvis made it clear that would not be happening and instead drafted Davey Faragher as bassist.

Even in these early days, Elvis wasn't sure he wanted to go back down the road of forming a permanent rock band again. He opted to record a solo album with Steve and Pete primarily assisting, though Elvis took on the lion's share of the drum programming and keyboard work, preferring his amateur touch to

Steve's refined hand. *When I Was Cruel*, released in April 2002, was touted as Elvis' first rock album 'since 199?'. An extensive live campaign followed, as did a series of albums – both with and without his new band (eventually christened The Imposters) – each exploring a wildly different mood and atmosphere to its predecessor. In fact, Elvis' work has become more ambitious over time: whether it's the plaintive torch songs of *North* (written about the failure of his marriage to Cait O'Riordan and eventual romantic rebirth with jazz musician Diana Krall, whom Elvis would marry in December 2003 – twin sons Dexter and Frank following three years later); the collaborative 2013 album, *Wise Up Ghost* (recorded with influential Philadelphia hip hop band and *Tonight Show* resident group, The Roots); or the lush, cinematic songscapes of *Look Now*, recorded to showcase The Imposters' many talents (Faragher, formerly of The Faragher Brothers and Low, is an impressive vocalist and arranger in addition to his equally impressive bass work).

Even in 2021, with the world still reeling from a global pandemic, Elvis has managed to be as productive as ever, recording and releasing the acclaimed *Hey Clockface*, and showing up as a surprise guest on Steve Nieve's innovative Immobile Tour. Elvis is still refining a follow-up album to *Painted From Memory* (two Costello/Bacharach co-writes slipped out on *Look Now*), and is planning several stage shows, including an adaptation of the 1957 film, *A Face In the Crowd* (about a con artist with political ambitions, who swindles an unsuspecting public, only to be brought down by a hot mic where he's caught deriding his followers). It's no coincidence that Elvis began work on the project in early 2016 when the world's political climate was only just beginning to resemble an overambitious screenwriter's fever dream.

Still, despite Elvis' continued output – critically beloved but commercially ignored – there are those fans who insist that his best work is behind him, preserved in amber and only reanimated when a quick buck is needed. (Witness the Elvis-curated – but ultimately disappointing – *Armed Forces* reissue of 2020, which offered only some incomplete live performances in addition to previously released outtakes and castoffs.) To those fans, I hope you enjoyed this book, but I also hope you'll give some of his later works a chance.

Resources and Further Reading

Books & Liner Notes

Costello, E., *Unfaithful Music and Disappearing Ink* (Blue Rider Press, 2016)
Costello, E., Liner notes for *My Aim Is True*, *This Year's Model*, *Armed Forces*, *Get Happy!!*, *Trust*, *Almost Blue*, *Imperial Bedroom*, *Punch the Clock*, *Goodbye Cruel World*, *King of America*, and *Blood & Chocolate* (Rykodisc, 1994–1995, and Rhino, 2001–2005)
Emerick, G. and Massey H., *Here, There and Everywhere: My Life Recording the Music of the Beatles* (Avery, 2006)
Gouldstone, D., *God's Comic* (St. Martin's Press, 1990)
Groothuizen, R. and den Heyer, K., *Going Through the Motions: Elvis Costello 1982–1985 (*Elcos, 1987)
Hilton, B., *Let Them All Talk* (Sanctuary, 1999)
Sheppard, D., *Elvis Costello* (*Kill Your Idols* series) (Thunder's Mouth Press, 2001)
Thomas, B., *The Big Wheel* (Helter Skelter Publishing, 2003 (reprint))
Thomson, G., *Complicated Shadows: The Life and Music of Elvis Costello* (Canongate Books Ltd, 2004)

Articles & interviews

Mulvey, J., *'The Ultimate Music Guide'* (Uncut, Jan, 2014)
Crawdaddy, (Mar. 1978)
Creem, (Feb. 1985)
Goldmine, (Dec. 1983)
Melody Maker, (27 Jul. 1985; 1 Mar. 1986; 22 Mar. 1986)
Musician, (Oct. 1983; Mar. 1986; Mar. 1994)
New Musical Express, (27 Aug. 1977; 9 Jun. 1979; 14 Feb. 1981; 30 Oct. 1982; 22 Feb. 1986; 1 Mar. 1986)
Record Mirror, (4 Apr. 1981; 8 Mar. 1986)
Rolling Stone, (2 Sep. 1982; 10 Apr. 1986)

Internet

www.elviscostello.com
wiki.elviscostello.info
facebook.com/ElvisCostello
h-online.co.uk/flipcity/flipcity.htm
clover-infopage.com
inanotherroom.com
stevenieve.com
nicklowe.net
tboneburnett.com
dianakrall.com

Compilations, Live Albums, and The Attractions' Solo' Album

The following is a brief run-through of compilations and live albums that represent the Attractions' output. Because it's nearly impossible to release an Elvis Costello compilation without the Attractions, his erstwhile band is well-represented, though many tend to drift towards the familiar. As a result, this will focus on the more interesting compilations to feature the band.

The live section is slimmer, as no live albums were released during the Attractions' tenures, something which Elvis would later lament as the band was such a force to be reckoned with onstage; this was remedied in the 1990s with archival live releases but, again, only releases of note will be mentioned.

The final section focuses on the Attractions' 'solo' album, *Mad About the Wrong Boy*.

Compilation Albums

Ten Bloody Marys & Ten How's Your Fathers (1980)

Much like The Who had released *Odds & Sods* to curb bootlegs of studio material that were appearing at an alarming rate, Elvis issued *Ten Bloody Marys & Ten How's Your Fathers* at the end of 1980 to collect B-sides and cast-offs that hadn't appeared on full-length studio albums, plus the three non-album singles, 'Watching The Detectives', 'Radio, Radio', and '(What's So Funny 'Bout) Peace, Love & Understanding?'. The title was a clever wink towards Elvis's Catholic upbringing, as well as a subtle nod towards his contemporary vices. Initially released on cassette only in the U.K. after imported copies of *Taking Liberties* started to filter in from the U.S., *Ten Bloody Marys* was eventually released on L.P. (and even CD in 1998).

Taking Liberties (1980)

The U.S. counterpart to *Ten Bloody Marys & Ten How's Your Fathers*, *Taking Liberties* took much of the same songs, with the exception of the aforementioned three non-album U.K. singles, here replaced by 'Night Rally', '(I Don't Want to Go to) Chelsea', and 'Sunday's Best', all of which had been removed from their respective U.S. albums for being 'too British'.

For a compilation of largely obscure material, *Taking Liberties* was relatively successful, reaching #28 in the U.S. The album was re-released on CD in 1995, with a bonus track (a live rendition of 'Psycho'), though both compilations have been made largely redundant by the many archival reissue series since 1993.

The Best of Elvis Costello & The Attractions (1985)

Released in the U.S. by Columbia Records when it became apparent that no new studio album was forthcoming in 1985 (in fact, Elvis was hard at work on *King Of America*), *The Best of Elvis Costello & The Attractions* was the first true compilation of their singles, and while the tracklisting may seem relatively standard and predictable by today's standards, it was, at the time, the perfect introduction to the vast and expansive career of Elvis (and the Attractions). The album, wrapped in a downright hideous sleeve of an amateurishly painted Elvis, peaked at a disappointing #116, though it finally achieved Gold status (sales of 500,000 or more) in November 1989 – just in time for the next Elvis Costello compilation album.

The Man (The Best of Elvis Costello) (1985)

Released in the U.K. and titled at the expense of Van' The Man' Morrison, this compilation album was the U.K. counterpart of *The Best of Elvis Costello & The Attractions*, with a drastically different tracklist and a companion video made up of all the promotional videos that had been filmed up until that point. The compilation was preceded by an extended remix of 'Green Shirt', which scraped into the U.K. charts at #68.

Out of Our Idiot (1987)

Much like *Taking Liberties* and *Ten Bloody Marys & Ten How's Your Fathers* in 1980, *Out of Our Idiot* was another roundup of B-sides, rarities, and unreleased outtakes that was released to bide time while Elvis worked on his new album. If anything, the compilation shows just how many alter egos Elvis possessed: in addition to his given stage name, songs were credited to the Coward Brothers, the Imposter, the Costello Show, the MacManus Gang, Napoleon Dynamite and the Royal Guard, and the Emotional Toothpaste. Whew!

While the album was a nice dumping ground for castoffs, it's also easy to see why the songs didn't make the cut the first time; unlike the first rarities compilations, which were received fairly well and featured material that some critics considered better than what Elvis was releasing at the time, *Out of Our Idiot* was largely ignored, though *Melody Maker* gave it a spin and called it 'a remarkable testament to how bloody unremarkable Elvis Costello can be when he puts his mind to it ... [But] it is not without its gold foil moments.' The album failed to chart and was skipped over for subsequent CD reissue campaigns, though it now is available to stream on Apple Music and Spotify.

Girls + £ ÷ Girls = $ & Girls (1989)

Another year, another compilation. Released at the end of 1989, just in time for the lucrative Christmas market, the bizarrely titled *Girls + £ ÷ Girls = $ & Girls* (itself a bastardisation of Elvis Presley's 1962 film) possesses a few things that previous compilations lacked. First, each format – cassette, vinyl, and CD – received a different tracklist from the other; second, Elvis himself penned the liner notes, often giving insightful meaning (or downright baffling explanations) to some of his most beloved songs; third, Elvis picked the running order, meaning that not only did he include the well-known 'hits', but he also threw in the occasional rarity. The songs were not organised chronologically but were 'arranged so as to tell a number of stories', as he wrote in the liners, with a mystery embedded in the album title.

Unfortunately, perhaps the most interesting of Elvis's compilations was destined to become obscure and was not remastered for CD in the 1990s. While it's worth tracking down solely for Elvis's liner notes, there are a few anomalies that don't exist elsewhere: the so-called 'U.K. version' of 'Uncomplicated' doesn't feature the clanging anvil effect after the line 'a horse that knows arithmetic', and the so-called single version of 'I Want You' is merely the album version shorn of a minute.

The Very Best of Elvis Costello & The Attractions (1994)

Featuring almost entirely singles released between 1977 and 1986, this compilation is rather predictable, with only a few surprising inclusions ('Watch Your Step' and 'Love Field', plus the two *King of America* selections), yet it still managed to reach #57 in the U.K.

Singles, Volumes 1-3 (2003)

Singles box sets were becoming quite the rage in the early 2000s, with any respectable artist or band issuing sets of their complete singles discography, complete with faithful reproductions of the singles sleeves and any overseas B-sides that might be an interesting inclusion for the die-hard fan – because these kinds of collections were, ultimately, for the fans.

Edsel Records collected Elvis's singles releases from 1977 to 1987 – covering the F-Beat/Demon and Columbia years – over three sets of twelve discs. On the surface, these sets are excellent and comprehensive, with informative liner notes from Alan Robinson, who takes care not to sound too much like a gushing fanboy, walking that fine line between congratulatory obsession and typical journalistic indifference.

But there are some catches: as Edsel is Elvis's U.K. equivalent of Rhino Records, then in charge of his back catalogue, the U.K. is represented more often than not, with US-only singles like 'This Year's Girl', 'Watch Your Step', and 'Lovable' not appearing anywhere. An equally curious absence is the 1985 remix of 'Green Shirt', which featured a legitimate extended version of the song; this may have been excluded from the release due to Elvis's apparent dislike of the remix, though that doesn't explain why remixes of other tracks appear here. (Or why 'Party Party', which Elvis has specifically pointed out as an embarrassment, is included.) In other cases, standard album versions of songs that featured special single remixes (such as 'Less Than Zero' and 'I Wanna Be Loved') are present, which makes the collection a little more frustrating. In some cases, previously unreleased material unintentionally made their appearances for the first time: 'Cry Cry Cry' and 'Wondering' both feature alternate vocal performances, and 'I Hope You're Happy Now', which should have been Elvis's solo version, was an otherwise unavailable version recorded with The Confederates. (The actual single versions of these songs appeared on the 2003 and 2005 CD reissues of *Almost Blue* and *King of America*, respectively.)

However, these are still worthwhile releases, though the campaign seems to have not extended beyond 1987 – a shame, as that's where Elvis's singles releases started to get even more interesting.

Live Albums

Live Stiffs (various artists; 1978)

Issued just as Elvis was preparing *This Year's Model* for release, the various artists live compilation *Live Stiffs* was culled from performances on the similarly-titled tour from October and November 1977. While Elvis had little affection for such a package tour, it did allow the rotating cast of the Stiff roster – including Nick Lowe, Ian Dury, Wreckless Eric, and Larry Wallis – a great deal of exposure.

Live Stiffs was released in February 1978, by which time Elvis's manager Jake Riviera had parted ways with Dave Robinson and Stiff, taking Elvis and Nick Lowe with him to Radar Records. This sampler album, then, served as a swan song for the first act of Stiff, just before Elvis and Nick would achieve greater success; subsequent Live Stiffs tours in 1978 and 1980 weren't as successful.

Each artist received two songs on the album (with the exception of Wallis, who got only one; instead, the tenth and final song was the obligatory all-star finale of Dury's 'Sex & Drugs & Rock & Roll'), though Elvis's were quite deliberately not hits: a cover of Burt Bacharach's 'I Just Don't Know What To Do With Myself' and *My Aim Is True* album track 'Miracle Man'. Understandably, a live sampler would have limited appeal to mainstream audiences, though this does a disserve to the actual performances, which perfectly capture the ramshackle and even combative attitudes of the tour. It's not pretty, but it does sum up Stiff Records quite well.

Live at El Mocambo (1978)

Elvis and the Attractions' gig at Toronto's El Mocambo club was recorded and broadcast live by local radio station CHUM-FM. The performance was so well-received that Elvis's Canadian record label distributed the recording as a limited edition promotional album, though that didn't stop it from becoming heavily bootlegged. It wouldn't be until 1993 that the album would receive its first official release as part of Rykodisc's *2 1/2 Years*, a four-disc box set that also collected Elvis's first three albums.

As for the performance itself, it's a startling revelation to hear how far The Attractions had progressed since their formation in July 1977: the performances are full of nervous tension and bottled-up energy, with the tight musicianship allowing Elvis to concentrate on his singing, only occasionally playing guitar (So intense are The Attractions, in particular the duelling talents of Bruce Thomas and Steve Nieve, that the listener hardly notices the absence of Elvis's guitar). The songs are short, concise, and masterfully executed, with barely any extraneous banter between Elvis and the audience; in fact, each song almost segues into the next, leaving the audience (and the listener) little chance to recover from the onslaught of the previous song.

Nick Lowe served as the opening act, and he returned to the stage shortly after the band, with Martin Belmont adding guitar on the finale, finished their fourteen song set (that included six old and eight newly recorded but still unreleased songs) to perform four of his own songs – 'Nutted By Reality', 'I Love The Sound Of Breaking Glass', 'Shake And Pop', and 'Heart Of The City' – with Elvis and The Attractions as his backup. These performances weren't released on *Live at El Mocambo*, presumably due to legal reasons, though they appeared as a separate Canadian promotional album that has yet to be released properly.

Live at Hollywood High (E.P.; 1979)

Released as a free giveaway with copies of *Armed Forces*, this trio of live performances from the exciting summer 1978 performance at Hollywood High School was the first widely available live release of Elvis and The Attractions. However, the brevity of the release, and the selection of songs – 'Accidents Will Happen', performed as a duet with Steve on piano and Elvis on vocal; 'Alison', a tender if not somewhat perfunctory rendition; and 'Watching The Detectives', the only really electrifying performance on the disc – meant that the true spirit of The Attractions as a live entity was not caught, and would have to be saved for another opportunity...

Live at Hollywood High (2010)

...such as the release of a full-length recording of the show. Rhino Records had released nine tracks (the three already available, and six additional tracks – 'Mystery Dance', 'Goon Squad', 'Party Girl', 'Stranger In The House', 'Lipstick Vogue', and 'You Belong To Me') on the 2002 *Armed Forces* deluxe edition, but it wouldn't be until 2010 when Hip-O Records released the full show as part of an archival live release campaign. Capturing the Attractions as a well-oiled machine, three months after the equally high-energy Mocambo gig, the quartet blast through a 20-song selection of hits and album tracks from the first two albums and three newly-written and unrecorded songs that would end up on *Armed Forces*. (Given the abundance of material already committed to plastic, including three unreleased songs in the set was pretty gutsy on Elvis's part; even more gutsy was opening the show with one of them.)

The Complete Armed Forces (2020)

Assembled during the COVID-19 lockdown that ravaged the world in 2020, *The Complete Armed Forces* collects outtakes and previously unreleased live performances to give as complete an overview of this period as was possible. Elvis mentioned in a September 2020 interview with *Billboard* that the box 'includes three live recordings ranging from the summer of '78 to the summer of '79, so it traces the development of the Attractions as a live act, from a club combo to a successful pop group – it's quite interesting to hear.'

While the alluringly-titled *Sketches for Emotional Fascism* – a 10" L.P. that contains 'Clean Money', 'Talking In The Dark', 'Wednesday Week', 'Tiny Steps',

'Crawling To The U.S.A.', 'Big Boys' (alternate version), 'Green Shirt' (demo version), and 'My Funny Valentine' – is a disappointment because the songs have long been available, the remaining four discs are more tantalising. *Riot at The Regent* captures The Attractions in Sydney, December 1978; *Europe '79 – Live at Pinkpop* is touted as being the full set (it's not – seven songs are missing); *Christmas in The Dominion* comes from a raucous set at London's Dominion Theatre; and *Live at Hollywood High & Elsewhere* collects nine songs from the already-released Hollywood High set and the solo rendition of 'Chemistry Class' from the 2002 CD reissue of *Armed Forces*.

While it's disappointing that the full live sets couldn't have been released, or that further studio or session outtakes weren't considered, *The Complete Armed Forces* is still a beautiful release, and is meant to be a visual experience, containing 'facsimiles of my original notebooks, all handwritten, lines scrawled out, half verses not used and all these subtle changes,' as Elvis told *Billboard*. 'It was a way of learning the songs as I wrote them, how to sing them, and also to understand the story the album told.'

The Attractions' 'Solo' Album
Mad About the Wrong Boy (1980)

In the same way that Crazy Horse recorded their eponymous album without their leader, Neil Young, The Attractions – minus Elvis – recorded their own album with the intention of releasing it as their first 'solo' album. In an attempt to show that they weren't merely hired hands, the trio wrote, sang, and performed (except guitar, which Bruce Thomas later revealed was his old Quiver bandmate Tim Renwick) sixteen of their own songs; three of them – 'Sad About Girls', 'Arms Race', and 'Damage' – were considered good enough to compete with Elvis's originals and were played live frequently in the late 1970s. 'Sad About Girls' was later recorded during sessions for *Trust* with Elvis on lead vocals, but it's likely that this momentary gesture of democracy was never seriously considered; Steve's song was discarded, and the suggestion that the others contribute material was never again made (or asked).

What emerged in September 1980 is a mixed bag: on the one hand, the trio is – as ever – rhythmically and melodically strong, turning in stellar musical performances with arrangements that certainly wouldn't have been out of place on any up-and-coming new wave act of the day. The one department that's a letdown is vocals: none of The Attractions were competent vocalists, but Steve Nieve was designated as the strongest vocalist for this occasion. The results are occasionally enjoyable, but mostly they're disconcerting: for fans who are accustomed to Elvis's customary croon, the anonymous voice that graces the sixteen tracks comes as a shock.

Lyrically, though, the songs are at least interesting, with The Attractions tackling such topical issues as nuclear war, conformity, boredom, self-loathing, and girls, girls, girls. Songwriting teams were divided into four groups: Steve Nieve wrote four songs on his own, while Bruce Thomas penned three. Bassist and drummer teamed up for both 'La La La La Loved You' and 'Lonesome Little Town', and the remainder were written by a curious duo dubbed Brain & Hart. It was later revealed that this was the pen name of Steve (as Brain) and his wife, Faye Hart. For reasons best known to Steve, he was periodically introduced onstage as Norman Brain around this time and was credited as Steve Hart on the *Trust* album.

Wrapped in a gauche and brightly-coloured sleeve, comprising of an obedient dog dutifully ignoring a delicious breakfast on a crimson shag rug, *Mad About the Wrong Boy* (or, as Elvis later dryly commented, *Too Clever by Two-Thirds*, indicating that he wasn't best pleased about the album release) is an interesting curio, but hardly worth repeated listens. The strongest tracks are 'Arms Race', 'La La La La Loved You', 'Single Girl', and 'Sad About Girls', and while there's nothing that's downright unlistenable, the album only reinforces the notion that The Attractions worked better as a backing band. It also didn't help that the album was recorded during a lull in their break-neck schedule of the summer of 1980; produced and engineered by Roger Bechirian at Eden Studios, the band had barely any time to think about the album before commencing work on *Trust*.

The Attractions remained fairly tight-lipped about the album in general, with only the ever-outspoken Bruce Thomas speaking about it. When *Guitar Player* asked him in 1987 if it was an experiment in flexing their creative muscles, the bassist laughed, 'Oh, hell. If it was flexing muscles, they were pretty puny muscles. All of those projects – I mean, The Rumour did it, and so did Spiders From Mars – and every time a band has ever done anything like that, they are doomed to failure. They never work. There were some good ideas on there, but it proved to me one thing: democracies don't work. Because by the time you please everybody, you dilute it three times over. If anybody heard the rehearsal things we did, it sounded like a much more dangerous version of the Bowie band. That was the kind of sound and approach we were going for. But everything went out the window. I think it would have been much better if we had actually played with a few different people. It would have been more interesting.'

The album was in and out of the shops fairly quickly, consigned to the bargain bins in stores that still carried it; surprisingly, two singles were extracted – 'Single Girl' backed with 'Slow Patience', released in July 1980, and 'Arms Race' backed with 'Lonesome Little Town', released in September 1980 (apparently, the most commercial track, 'La La La La Loved You', wasn't even considered) – which, much like the album, hardly made a dent in the charts.

Also from Sonicbond

On Track series

Barclay James Harvest – Keith and Monica Domone 978-1-78952-067-5
The Beatles – Andrew Wild 978-1-78952-009-5
The Beatles Solo 1969-1980 – Andrew Wild 978-1-78952-030-9
Blue Oyster Cult – Jacob Holm-Lupo 978-1-78952-007-1
Kate Bush – Bill Thomas 978-1-78952-097-2
The Clash – Nick Assirati 978-1-78952-077-4
Crosby, Stills and Nash – Andrew Wild 978-1-78952-039-2
Deep Purple and Rainbow 1968-79 – Steve Pilkington 978-1-78952-002-6
Dire Straits – Andrew Wild 978-1-78952-044-6
Dream Theater – Jordan Blum 978-1-78952-050-7
Emerson Lake and Palmer – Mike Goode 978-1-78952-000-2
Fairport Convention – Kevan Furbank 978-1-78952-051-4
Genesis – Stuart MacFarlane 978-1-78952-005-7
Gentle Giant – Gary Steel 978-1-78952-058-3
Hawkwind – Duncan Harris 978-1-78952-052-1
Iron Maiden – Steve Pilkington 978-1-78952-061-3
Jethro Tull – Jordan Blum 978-1-78952-016-3
Elton John in the 1970s – Peter Kearns 978-1-78952-034-7
Gong – Kevan Furbank 978-1-78952-082-8
Iron Maiden – Steve Pilkington 978-1-78952-061-3
Judas Priest – John Tucker 978-1-78952-018-7
Kansas – Kevin Cummings 978-1-78952-057-6
Aimee Mann – Jez Rowden 978-1-78952-036-1
Joni Mitchell – Peter Kearns 978-1-78952-081-1
The Moody Blues – Geoffrey Feakes 978-1-78952-042-2
Mike Oldfield – Ryan Yard 978-1-78952-060-6
Queen – Andrew Wild 978-1-78952-003-3
Renaissance – David Detmer 978-1-78952-062-0
The Rolling Stones 1963-80 – Steve Pilkington 978-1-78952-017-0
Steely Dan – Jez Rowden 978-1-78952-043-9
Thin Lizzy – Graeme Stroud 978-1-78952-064-4
Toto – Jacob Holm-Lupo 978-1-78952-019-4
U2 – Eoghan Lyng 978-1-78952-078-1
UFO – Richard James 978-1-78952-073-6
The Who – Geoffrey Feakes 978-1-78952-076-7
Roy Wood and the Move – James R Turner 978-1-78952-008-8
Van Der Graaf Generator – Dan Coffey 978-1-78952-031-6
Yes – Stephen Lambe 978-1-78952-001-9
Frank Zappa 1966 to 1979 – Eric Benac 978-1-78952-033-0
10CC – Peter Kearns 978-1-78952-054-5

Decades Series

Pink Floyd In The 1970s – Georg Purvis 978-1-78952-072-9
Marillion in the 1980s – Nathaniel Webb 978-1-78952-065-1

Other Books

Derek Taylor: For Your Radioactive Children – Andrew Darlington
978-1-78952-

Jon Anderson and the Warriors - the road to Yes – David Watkinson
978-1-78952-059-0

Tommy Bolin: In and Out of Deep Purple – Laura Shenton
978-1-78952-070-5

Maximum Darkness – Deke Leonard 978-1-78952-048-4
Maybe I Should've Stayed In Bed – Deke Leonard 978-1-78952-053-8
The Twang Dynasty – Deke Leonard 978-1-78952-049-1

Would you like to write for Sonicbond Publishing?

We are mainly a music publisher, but we also occasionally publish in other genres including film and television. At Sonicbond Publishing we are always on the look-out for authors, particularly for our two main series, On Track and Decades.

Mixing fact with in depth analysis, the On Track series examines the entire recorded work of a particular musical artist or group. All genres are considered from easy listening and jazz to 60s soul to 90s pop, via rock and metal.

The Decades series singles out a particular decade in an artist or group's history and focuses on that decade in more detail than may be allowed in the On Track series.

While professional writing experience would, of course, be an advantage, the most important qualification is to have real enthusiasm and knowledge of your subject. First-time authors are welcomed, but the ability to write well in English is essential.

Sonicbond Publishing has distribution throughout Europe and North America, and all our books are also published in E-book form. Authors will be paid a royalty based on sales of their book. Further details about our books are available from www.sonicbondpublishing.com. To contact us, complete the contact form there or email info@sonicbondpublishing.co.uk